morning garden

Comes to Your Table

125 Recipes
Reflecting the Four Seasons

Lucy Mercer and the Morning Garden Moms

To all our moms:

The most beautiful women in the world.

Distributed in the United Stated by Hands Together Center for Children
201 East Civic Center Drive
Santa Ana, California 92701

www.handstogether-sa.org

The mission of Hands Together is to provide the highest quality early
education and care to working poor families who are striving to gain
stability, improve their lives, and emerge from poverty.

A portion of the proceeds of the sale of this book will be donated
to support the work of Hands-Together's Morning Garden program.

Cover design by Rhonda Priestley

ISBN 978-0-615-62134-0

Printed by Alphagraphics in Irvine, CA
First Edition

Contents

WINTER

PROFILES

SPRING

I was hungry and you gave me food,
I was thirsty and you gave me drink,
I was a stranger and you welcomed me.

MATTHEW 25:35

Acknowledgements

Four years ago my friend, Carol Griset, launched an expansion of the Morning Garden program that swept me into the heart of Santa Ana. There, in the parish kitchen of the Episcopal Church of the Messiah, a handful of homeless Santa Ana women and I started to cook. Since then, a steady stream of changing hands, hearts, and faces has made its way through the kitchen, and we've created thousands of family-style meals along the way.

My gratitude expands to include each and every one of our Morning Garden moms, as well as the children, the sprinkling of dads, the steadfast staff, the constant trickle of guests and enthusiastic volunteers, and our stalward supporters The Marisal Foundation as well as the Sisters of Saint Joseph of Orange. All, in their turn, have made the planning, the shopping, the cooking, and the eating a blessed and joyful event.

Over the years I have inevitably relied heavily on the knowledge, goodwill, and kindness of many others who will have to remain nameless here, simply because of the short circuitry within my human memory. However, a few names stand out. And I know for a fact that our bountiful Wednesday meals would have been far more meager and this book would never have seen the light of day, without the ready guidance, and the technical and financial support from the following generous souls.

Thank you: David Mercer, Ann Campbell, Toni Mendoza, Mary Butler, Cristina Damian, Pam Fuller, Thomas Miller, Mike Jones, Susan Martin, Klaus Stobbe, Susana Dorfman, Mary Anderson, and Kathy Kipp. As for Linda Calkins: You're the best.

Introduction

"Morning Garden Comes to Your Table" is a cookbook of menus organized by the four seasons. The whole collection contains 30 menus, each menu containing three to five simple-to-follow recipes. Though many of the recipes reflect some seasonal restriction, you'll find that there's quite a bit of overlap and many of the recipes are suited to any time of the year.

OUR PROCESSES AND EQUIPMENT

You'll also find that this is not a book expounding long processes with sourdough breads, stocks, croissants, and multi layered cakes; we stick with what's achievable with a few ingredients undergoing a bit of chopping and a few minutes of cooking. Chopping might, in fact, be the only culinary skill required. And, other than a knife with a keen edge, the only other "special" equipment required is a cutting board. Of course, you'll also need a stove, a skillet, a pot, a spatula and a spoon.

For cakes and cookies, we like to use parchment paper to line our baking sheets because that way, on the few occasions that we've gone beyond "golden brown," the cleanup has always been—well, easier than pie. For salad dressings, creamy sauces, and soups, we find that we're always reaching for an immersion blender, our one and only "fancy" kitchen tool that's attached to an electric cord.

OUR PANTRY

Since we cook in a church kitchen, our pantry consists of a box of salt, a shaker of pepper, an assembly of hot sauces, a tin of sugar, as well as the odds and ends left over from functions ranging from the all-church pancake breakfast to the daily after-school teen program Noah's Project. Still, within those meager pickings, culinary discoveries have been made. Brown sugar brings a nuanced sweetness to whipped cream toppings; soy sauce imparts notes of *umami* to a lack-luster soup; cookies can be made with just three ingredients: a cup of peanut butter, a cup of sugar and one egg.

SEVERAL FAVORITE THINGS

Salt

We keep a small bowl of salt at hand and sprinkle all our dishes lightly at the beginning of the cooking process and again, after tasting, at the end. No other single thing has enhanced our cooking efforts as much as the judicious use of this kitchen staple.

Garlic

To our mind, you can't go wrong with fresh garlic. We either slice it paper thin or mash it with a bit of salt with the back of a spoon or in a mortar with a pestle and stir it into salads, and soups, and anything stir fried.

Lemon

Unlike malodorous garlic, lemon smells sparklingly bright. But, just like garlic, lemon has the power to transform the boring into something exciting. We use the grated zest in many of our desserts. As for the juice, we frequently put it in salad dressings and always sprinkle it on apples, bananas, and avocados to keep them from turning brown.

Fresh herbs

We grow pots of fresh herbs in several sunny spots in the church courtyard where, with our southern California year-long growing season, we always have plenty of parsley, thyme, chives, and coriander on hand. At the entrance to the church office stands a bushy rosemary shrub that some kind soul planted years ago; during our winters we gratefully chop these pointy leaves fine and sprinkle them over our roasted vegetables and meats.

HOW TO USE THIS BOOK

At Morning Garden, we serve menus consisting of three to five separate family-style dishes. We always make enough food to feed at least thirty people. And we make the complete meal within 90 minutes. The menus and recipes in this book reflect much of what we have learned along our journey of serving seasonal, made-from-scratch food fast. When cooking with the recipes found in this book, please always keep in mind that they are only road maps of where we at Morning Garden have found success over the years.

So, in the spirit of fun and adventure, always feel free to exclude or recombine ingredients in any of our recipes in ways that will reflect the tastes of your own family and guests. After all, the goal we cooks have in common is to set a table with food that everyone will eat—maybe not love, but at least will give everyone the opportunity to taste and to participate in the fellowship of breaking bread at the table.

OUR PHILOSOPHY

Though our cupboards are often scantly stocked, and our techniques and equipment basic at best, we passionately choose to cook from scratch and consistently strive to reflect the seasons: beans and apricots in summer; pumpkin and cranberries in fall; pecans and oranges in winter; asparagus and strawberries in spring. Since we always have substantial numbers of children eating at the Morning Garden table, there are certain foods we have never served; hence, in this book, you'll find no recipes for anything with anchovies, sea urchins, clams, pickles, okra, or lard.

An overriding philosophy to keep in mind, when cooking out of this book, is to pursue fresh and seasonal ingredients and to involve the whole family in the shopping, the cooking, the sitting, the eating, and the sharing at the family table.

Lucy Mercer
Spring 2012

Summer

apricots

beans, green

blackberries

cherries

corn

cucumbers

eggplant

grapes

herbs

limes

melons

peaches

peppers

squash, summer

tomatoes

vegetables, leafy green

SUMMER BRUNCH

Morning Garden French Toast

Fruit Kebabs

Hash Brown Sausage Casserole

Spinach Salad with Strawberries

Baked Rhubarb

Shortbread Cookies

Morning Garden French Toast

One of the reasons all of us at Morning Garden love this French toast is that the filling always reminds us of cheesecake. The other plus is that it's really easy to make.

SERVINGS: Enough for 6

FRENCH TOAST

12 slices of bread, any kind on hand
1/2 cup cottage cheese
1 tablespoon sour cream
1-2 tablespoons sugar
Pinch of lemon peel, grated fine
3 eggs
2 tablespoons whipping cream
Butter for browning

FRUIT KEBABS

Thread pieces of seasonal fruit on bamboo skewers. Brush with your favorite jam, melted in the microwave oven with a bit of water stirred in.

WHAT TO DO:

1. Mix cottage cheese with sour cream, sugar and lemon peel.

2. Spread the cottage cheese mixture between two pieces of bread to make sandwiches. Refrigerate until ready to cook.

3. Melt some butter in a skillet and heat up to the point when it stops foaming.

4. Combine the eggs with whipping cream, and carefully soak the sandwiches in the egg mixture. Arrange them in the hot skillet and brown on each side.

5. Keep warm in a 200-degree oven until ready to eat. Serve cut into wedges with maple syrup and fruit kebabs.

Hash Brown Sausage Casserole

You could throw this together the night before and keep it in the refrigerator to bake in the morning. Or, it's equally good made right away.

SERVINGS: Enough for 6

1 pound ground pork sausage
1 onion, chopped
6 eggs, beaten
2 tablespoons flour
1/2 cup sour cream
1/2 cup scallions, chopped
1 tablespoon fresh thyme
1/2 teaspoon salt
2 cups frozen hash brown potatoes, defrosted
1/2 cup cheddar cheese, shredded

WHAT TO DO:

1. Butter a ceramic casserole dish, and preheat the oven to 325 degrees.

2. In a large skillet, brown the sausage. When done, spoon the browned sausage out of the skillet into a bowl.

3. Brown the chopped onion in the same skillet, and add to the bowl with the sausage.

4. Reserving the cheese, mix the rest of the ingredients into the bowl with the sausage and onions.

5. Pour mixture out into buttered baking dish, sprinkle with the cheese, and bake until puffy and golden—about 30 minutes.

Spinach Salad with Strawberries

A large bowl of salad greens combined with sliced fruit of any kind is always exciting to behold and delightful to eat.

SERVINGS: Enough for 6

VINAIGRETTE
1/2 cup rice vinegar
1/4 cup sugar
2 tablespoons onion, chopped
2 teaspoons Dijon Mustard
1/2 cup strawberries, chopped
1 cup vegetable oil

SALAD
1 pound baby spinach
1 cup strawberries, sliced thin

WHAT TO DO:

1. Blend all the vinaigrette ingredients with an immersion blender.

2. Let the flavors combine for several hours at room temperature.

3. Strain through a fine strainer into a jar, and keep refrigerated for use as needed.

4. Mix spinach with desired amount of dressing in a large bowl.

5. Sprinkle strawberries over the top, and serve.

Baked Rhubarb Compote

Rhubarb has a short season. But what an exuberant burst of lip-smacking-good flavor!

SERVINGS: Enough for 6

3 cups rhubarb, cut into 1-inch piece
1 cup brown sugar
1/4 teaspoon cinnamon

WHAT TO DO:

1. Preheat oven to 350 degrees.

2. Combine rhubarb with sugar and cinnamon, and bake for 30 minutes in a porcelain casserole dish.

3. Take out of the oven, stir to combine and let cool before serving.

TIP: We like this compote as is, but it only improves when served with a couple of shortbread cookies.

Shortbread Cookies

The secret to the irresistible crunchy and at the same time tender texture of this cookie is the rice flour.

SERVINGS: Makes 20-30 cookies, depending of size

1 pound butter
3 cups flour
1 cup rice flour
Pinch of salt
1 cup powdered sugar
Any flavor jam

WHAT TO DO:

1. With a mixer, cream the butter along with the sugar until fluffy.

2. Add the flours and mix to combine.

3. Shape the dough into a big disk and refrigerate for one hour.

4. When ready to bake, roll walnut-sized pinches of cookie dough into balls. Arrange on a cookie sheet lined with parchment paper.

5. Press each cookie flat to a ½-inch thickness with the bottom of a glass, make a thumb print indentation into each cookie and fill it with a dot of jam (no more than ¼ teaspoon).

6. Bake at 325 degrees for 15 minutes.

KIDS' BIRTHDAY PARTY

Skillet Meatball Pizza

Caesar Salad with Watermelon

Bethany's Instant Birthday Cupcakes

Skillet Meatball Pizza

On a base of store-bought refrigerated biscuits, scatter some mini meatballs, sprinkle on some fresh basil, oregano and Parmesan cheese, top with a thick coating of Mozzarella and every one will think you're a pizza genius.

SERVINGS: Enough for six hearty eaters

PIZZA DOUGH
1 container of your favorite, pre-made refrigerated biscuits

MEATBALL-TOMATO SAUCE
1/2 pound ground beef
1/2 pound ground pork
1 egg, lightly beaten
Salt and pepper
1/2 cup bread crumbs
2 tablespoons oil
1 1/2 cups store-bought tomato sauce

TOPPING
1/3 cup julienned fresh basil
1 1/2 tablespoons fresh oregano leaves (2 teaspoons dried)
1/2 cup grated Parmesan cheese
3 cups shredded mozzarella cheese

WHAT TO DO:

1. Make a mixture of the beef, pork, and egg. Season with salt and pepper, and shape into small meatballs.

2. Roll meatballs in the bread crumbs to cover with an even coating. (Can be kept refrigerated for up to several hours before browning.)

3. Heat oil in skillet, and brown the meatballs on all sides, 5-6 minutes per batch.

4. Pour the tomato sauce over the meatballs and simmer for 5 to 7 minutes.

5. Cool the meatball-tomato sauce to room temperature.

PUTTING IT ALL TOGETHER:

1. Preheat the oven to 400 degrees for 20 minutes.

2. Split each unbaked biscuit horizontally into two halves and arrange them to more or less cover the bottom of two oven-safe skillets. Don't worry about leaving some space between the biscuits.

3. Spread about ½ cup of meatball-tomato sauce over the dough.

4. Sprinkle with the basil, oregano and Parmesan cheese; scatter each pizza with final topping of 1 cup of the mozzarella cheese.

5. Bake until the crust is crisp and the cheese is bubbly, about 15 minutes. Remove from oven. Remember that the handle will be hot.

6. Let cool for 5 minutes. Cut or pull apart and serve.

TIP: For some tasty appetizer-size munching, press the split biscuits lightly into muffin pans, and top each with a meatball, two teaspoons of sauce, as well a sprinkling of any cheese combo on hand. Bake for 15 minutes in a 400-degree oven. Cool for 5 minutes before taking out of the pan.

Caesar Salad with Watermelon

Chunks of watermelon scattered about the lettuce gives this perennial favorite a summery twist. We make our own dressing too: With an immersion blender, it's truly a snap to make.

FOR THE SALAD

Romaine lettuce, wash and tear into bite-size pieces.
Cut the watermelon into small chunks and scatter over the lettuce.

FOR THE CAESAR SALAD DRESSING

2/3 cup oil
1/3 cup vinegar (or a half-and-half combination of vinegar and lemon juice)
1 teaspoon salt
2 garlic cloves
2 tablespoons Parmesan cheese, grated

PUTTING IT ALL TOGETHER:

1. Blend the salad dressing ingredients together with an immersion blender.

2. Pour salad dressing, to taste, over the lettuce and watermelon.

3. Mix gently. Sprinkle with fresh ground pepper, before serving.

Bethany's Instant Birthday Cupcakes

We can't think of anything easier to whip up for a birthday treat than these no-bake cupcakes. And they taste great too!

YOU WILL NEED:

Small clear plastic cups
Half of a Pound Cake—we bought ours at the super market
1-2 cups Whipping Cream
Sugar to taste
Fresh Fruit—we used peeled Peaches and Blueberries
A few drops of Lemon Juice—to keep the fruit looking fresh
Bought candy for decoration
Candles

WHAT TO DO:

1. Peel and cut fruit into small pieces and stir in some sugar and lemon juice. To maximize the flavor, leave the mixed fruit out at room temperature. (This step can be completed an hour or two before assembling the cupcakes.)

2. Whip the cream and sugar to taste with an electric mixer.

3. Cut the pound cake into small cubes and combine with the whipped cream.

4. Place a layer of fruit in the bottom of the plastic cup.

5. Cover fruit with the cake and whipped cream combination.

6. Decorate with candy. (We chose our candy to look like mini fruit—to keep with our summer theme.)

7. Light the candles and make a wish.

Morning Garden Comes to Your Table

FAMILY FRIENDLY EATING

Sloppy Joe Sandwiches
Creamed Corn
Cabbage and Fennel Slaw
Lemon Icebox Cake Parfait

Sloppy Joe's

SERVINGS: Enough for 4 sandwiches

1 pound ground beef or turkey, or a mixture of both
1 small onion, minced
1 tablespoon oil
1 cup catsup
1/3 cup water
1/4 cup brown sugar
1 tablespoon mustard
1 tablespoon Worchestershire sauce
Vinegar to taste (at least 2 tablespoons)
Salt and pepper
Hamburger Buns

WHAT TO DO:

1. Heat the skillet with the oil and sauté the onion for about five minutes.

2. Spoon the sauted onion out of the skillet and reserve it in a bowl. Reheat the same skillet, without washing it, sauté the beef until well browned—this will take up to 10 minutes.

3. While the meat is browning, combine the remaining ingredients with the sauted onions in the bowl.

4. Blend all ingredients into a smooth sauce with an immersion blender, add to the beef in the skillet, and heat thoroughly.

Serve on hamburger buns.

Creamed Corn

The secret to the extraordinary flavor of this simple preparation is the fresh corn.

SERVINGS: Enough for 4

8 ears of corn
1 tablespoon butter
1 tablespoon half and half
Salt
Cayenne pepper

WHAT TO DO:

1. Husk the corn.

2. Grate each ear of corn with a hand grater directly into a baking dish.

3. Bake at 350 degrees for 20 minutes.

4. Take out of the oven and stir in the butter, cream, salt and cayenne pepper.

5. Keep warm until ready to serve.

TIP: Frozen corn can be used as a successful substitute here. Just pour some solidly frozen corn into the food processor, pulse a few times to make a coarse mush, and proceed with the recipe.

Cabbage and Fennel Slaw

We always try to make our basic coleslaw more colorful as well as more flavorful with the addition of some surprise veggies. Here we added thin slices of fennel and grated in some carrots.

SERVINGS: Enough for 6

FOR THE DRESSING
1/4 cup mayonnaise
1 tablespoon lemon juice
1 teaspoon grated orange peel
1 teaspoon sugar
1/2 teaspoon fennel seeds, crushed
1 jalapeno pepper, minced
Salt and pepper

FOR THE VEGGIES
2 cups cabbage—a mixture of red and green, shredded
1 fennel bulb, sliced paper thin
2 carrots, grated
4 scallions, sliced thinly on the diagonal
4 bacon strips, fried and crumbled
1/4 cup Feta cheese

WHAT TO DO:

1. Mix the dressing ingredients together.

2. Pour the dressing over the veggies and mix in a large bowl.

3. Top with crumbled bacon and Feta cheese.

Lemon Icebox Cake Parfait

When we couldn't locate a serrated knife up to the challenge of cutting our baked cake into horizontal layers, we ended cutting the cake into chunks and creating a parfait instead of our intended layered icebox cake.

SERVINGS: Enough for 8

1 baked round of vanilla flavored cake
2 cups whipping cream
1/4 cup confectioners' sugar
1 cup Lemon Curd (store bought or home made)
1/2 cup blueberries
Mint leaves
Drinking cups

WHAT TO DO:

1. Cut cake into ½-inch chunks.

2. Whip cream with sugar.

3. Combine whipped cream with Lemon Curd.

4. Layer cake with cream in clear drinking cups, ending with a swirl of lemony whipped cream.

5. Top with a few blueberries and a mint leaf.

6. Keep refrigerated until ready to serve.

COLORFUL SUMMER LUNCH

Apricot Chicken Kebabs
Tarragon Green Bean Salad
Arugula, Orange, Red Onion & Feta Salad
Yogurt Dressing with Dukkah
Chocolaty Oatmeal Cookies
Strawberries

Apricot Chicken Kebabs

You can fry the chicken yourself or doctor up some store bought fried chicken into these tasty, neat bundles.

SERVINGS: Enough for 4

FOR THE CHICKEN
1 pound chicken thighs with skin
5 tablespoons cornstarch
5 tablespoons flour
1/2 teaspoon salt
Pinch of cayenne pepper
Vegetable oil for frying

WHAT TO DO:

1. Debone the chicken thighs and cut each piece into 6 smaller pieces.

2. Dust all the chicken pieces with a mixture of cornstarch, four, salt, and cayenne pepper.

3. Fry chicken in hot oil until crisp and done (about 5 minutes).

4. Drain the fried chicken on paper towels.

TO MAKE THE KEBABS
1/4 cup apricot preserves
Drops of chili oil, to taste
Soft lettuce leaves for wrapping the chicken
Mini tomatoes

1. Heat the preserves in the microwave until warm. Stir in a few drops of chili oil.

2. Brush the fried chicken pieces with the melted preserves.

3. Wrap each piece in a lettuce leaf.

4. Alternating with the tomatoes, thread the lettuce-wrapped chicken onto bamboo skewers.

TIP: Serve the kebabs as is, or with a dipping sauce made with 3 tablespoons soy sauce, 1 tablespoon lemon juice, ½ teaspoon of chili paste, a touch of sugar and a sprinkling of chopped cilantro.

Tarragon Green Bean Salad

1 pound green beans
2 tablespoons any oil-and-vinegar dressing
1 tablespoon fresh tarragon, chopped fine

WHAT TO DO:

1. Boil the green beans in plenty of salted water for 5-10 minutes.

2. When done to taste, pour the beans into a colander.

3. Dunk the hot beans into a bowl of ice water until they're icy cold.

4. Drain again and mix with the dressing.

5. Sprinkle with tarragon and refrigerate until ready to use.

TIP: Draining the beans first in a colander, then plunging them into a bowl of icy water, stops further cooking and keeps the color bright green.

Arugula, Orange, Red Onion & Feta Salad

SERVINGS: Enough for 6

7-ounce bag of arugula
2 oranges, peeled and sliced
1/2 red onion, sliced paper thin
1/4 pound Feta cheese, crumbled

WHAT TO DO:

1. On a bed of arugula, arrange the orange slices with the onion.

2. Sprinkle with Feta cheese.

3. Serve, topped with the yogurt dressing and Dukkah.

TIP: We are never disappointed with the taste of Bulgarian Feta.

Yogurt Dressing with Dukkah

The following recipe for Dukkah, an Egyptian nut and spice mixture, came to our notice via Cristina Damian who sometimes volunteers her time in the Morning Garden kitchen. Cristina says that she uses this mixture to enhance the flavor of almost everything: Sprinkled on bread, dipped in olive oil; on salads; on baked chicken; on stir-frys. We love it on everything too--especially everything that contains yogurt such as our yogurt dressing.

FOR THE DRESSING
Mix ½ cup of store-bought Italian style dressing with 2 tablespoons yogurt. Refrigerate until ready to use.

FOR THE DUKKAH

1/3 cup pistachios
1/3 cup almonds
1/3 cup sesame seeds
2 tablespoons coriander seeds
2 tablespoons cumin seeds
2 tablespoons freshly ground black pepper
1 teaspoon flaked sea salt

WHAT TO DO:

1. Preheat the oven to 350 degrees F.

2. Place the pistachios and almonds on a baking sheet, and bake for about five minutes, or until fragrant.

3. While the nuts are still hot, dump them out on tea towel. Fold the towel over, and rub the baked nuts to remove the skins. Set aside to cool.

4. In a dry skillet over medium heat, toast the sesame seeds until light golden brown; pour into a bowl, to cool.

5. In the same skillet, toast the coriander and cumin seeds while shaking the pan or stirring occasionally until they begin to pop. Transfer the spices into a food processor (a blended works here too) and process until finely ground.

6. Combine the ground spices with the sesame seeds in a bowl.

7. Place the cooled almonds and pistachios into the food processor, and pulse into a coarse flour.

8. Stir in the spices and sesame seeds. Season with salt and pepper.

TIP: Store the dukkah in an airtight container, and enjoy it sprinkled on everything—especially on Pita bread, first dipped into warmed olive oil.

Chocolaty Oatmeal Cookies with Strawberries

No need to get out the mixer to make this wonderfully easy cookie dough. Just plan to let it rest in the refrigerator over-night, or even several days.

SERVINGS: Makes 40 large cookies

1 cup flour
2 cups old-fashioned oatmeal (not quick cooking)
1/2 teaspoon baking powder
1/2 teaspoon baking soda
1 teaspoon cinnamon
1/2 teaspoon salt
1 cup vegetable shortening
1 1/2 cup sugar, either brown or white (we use a mixture of both)
1 teaspoon vanilla
2 eggs
1 cup pecans, chopped fine
Chocolate chips—to melt and pour over baked cookies

WHAT TO DO:

1. In a large bowl, stir together the flour, oatmeal, baking soda, cinnamon and salt.

2. Melt the shortening in a saucepan.

3. Stir the sugar into the melted shortening, follow with the vanilla and eggs.

4. Combine the melted shortening mixture with the dry ingredients in a large bowl and stir just until everything is equally moist. Stir in the nuts.

5. Place the dough into a Ziploc bag and refrigerate overnight.

6. When ready to bake the cookies, preheat the oven to 350 degrees.

7. For large cookies, scoop out about 2 tablespoons of dough, and roll into balls on a plate covered with cinnamon sugar--made with about 1 teaspoon cinnamon mixed with ¼ cup white sugar.

8. Arrange cookies about 3 inches apart on the cookie sheet. Flatten each cookie slightly with the bottom of a glass, and bake for 15 minutes.

9. When cool, pour several crisscrossed lines over the top with melted chocolate. Serve with strawberries.

TIP: Using shortening instead of butter lets the oatmeal taste shine brightly in each bite.

FINGER LICKING GOOD MEAL

Crispy Fried Chicken

Zucchini Pancakes

Herb Pesto

Tomato-Cucumber Salad

Inside-Out Carrot-Cake Cookies

Crispy Fried Chicken

SERVINGS: Enough for 6

3 pounds bone-in chicken thighs
1/2 cup honey
3 tablespoons lemon juice
2 eggs
1 tablespoon soy sauce
1/2 cup four
1/2 cup cornstarch
1/4 cup cornmeal
1 teaspoon salt
1/4 teaspoon cayenne pepper
1 cup oil

WHAT TO DO:

1. In a large bag combine chicken with the honey and lemon juice. Refrigerate for at least 3 hours or overnight.

2. Blend the two eggs with the soy sauce in a bowl.

3. In another dish, mix the remaining dry ingredients.

4. Take the chicken out of the bag and dip each piece first into the egg mixture, then coat with the flour.

5. Let the chicken pieces dry out at room temperature for about 30 minutes, before frying them golden done in hot oil.

TIP: Alas, we don't always have it in our pantry, but we always agree that we like the taste of fried chicken best when we use Peanut Oil.

Zucchini Pancakes

SERVINGS: Enough for 6

1 1/2 pounds zucchini
1 teaspoon salt
1/4 cup onion
1 egg
1/2 cup bread crumbs
Vegetable oil for frying

WHAT TO DO:

1. Grate zucchini on a large-holed grater or in a food processor. Sprinkle with salt, mix, and drain in a colander for 30 minutes--along the way, pressing out any excess moisture as it seeps out of the vegetable.

2. Chop the onion into small pieces and sauté for 5-7 minutes in a hot skillet with a bit of oil.

3. Place the cooked onion in a bowl, to cool.

4. Combine the onion with the egg, the drained zucchini, and the bread crumbs. Mix everything lightly into a batter.

5. When ready to fry, drop about 2 tablespoons of zucchini batter into a hot, oil-filmed skillet.

6. Flatten pancakes with a spatula to ¼-inch thicknesses and fry on both sides until done.

7. Keep warm in 200-degree oven until ready to serve. Serve with any green, herby pesto or a salsa.

Herbed Pesto

SERVINGS: Makes about 1 cup

1/2 cup pine nuts or walnuts nuts, toasted
1 1/2 cup fresh basil
1/2 cup Italian parsley
1/4 cup tarragon
2 cloves garlic
Pinch of dried chili peppers
Pinch of salt
1/3 cup vegetable oil

WHAT TO DO:

Blend all ingredients in a food processor or with an immersion blender.
Pour into a jar with a lid and refrigerate. Use as a topping for pretty much
anything that might need a boost of flavor.

Tomato-Cucumber Salad

SERVINGS: Enough for 6

3 tomatoes, diced
1 cucumber, sliced paper thin
3 spring onions, sliced thin on an oblique angle
1 tablespoon Balsamic vinegar
Salt and pepper

WHAT TO DO:

1. Combine onions with tomatoes. Season with vinegar and salt and pepper.

2. In another bowl, sprinkle the cucumbers lightly with salt.

3. When ready to serve, gently squeeze the accumulated water out of the
cucumbers and combine them with the tomatoes and onions.

Inside-Out Carrot-Cake Cookies

To make these cookies inside out, we take two cookies and sandwich them with a simple icing made with 8 ounces of cream cheese and 1/4 cup honey.

SERVINGS: Makes about 12 filled cookies

1 1/4 cups flour
1 teaspoon cinnamon
1 teaspoon baking powder
1 teaspoon baking soda
1/2 teaspoon salt
1 cup sugar
2/3 cup vegetable oil
2 egg
1 1/2 cups shredded carrots
1/2 cup canned, crushed pineapple (well drained)
1/2 cup walnuts, toasted and chopped
1/2 cup raisins

WHAT TO DO:

1. Preheat oven to 375 degrees.

2. Beat the sugar, oil, and eggs in a standing mixer for about 3 minutes—until light in texture and color.

3. Reduce the mixer speed to slow and add the flour, cinnamon, salt, and baking powder and soda. Mix until just combined. Into the batter, hand stir the carrots, pineapple, nuts and raisins.

5. Drop 1 1/2 tablespoons of batter, two inches apart, on greased cookie sheets. Bake for about 15 minutes, until lightly browned.

6. When completely cool, spread any cream cheese icing between two cookies, or use the one that's printed at the beginning of this cookie recipe.

SUNNY BURGER LUNCH

Lamb Burgers with Minty Sauce

Summer Green Risotto

Glazed Carrots

Honey-Apricot Parfait

Lamb Burgers with Minty Sauce

To make the yogurt for the sauce thicker and more like Greek yogurt, pour off any liquid gathered on top before stirring and spooning the yogurt out of its container.

SERVINGS: Enough for 6

FOR THE SAUCE
1 cup plain yogurt
1 cup fresh mint leaves
1 teaspoon fresh lemon juice
1 garlic clove

FOR THE BURGERS
1 1/2 pounds lamb, ground
3 sprigs rosemary, minced
2 garlic cloves, minced
1/4 cup Italian parsley, minced
1/4 cup onion, minced
1/2 teaspoon salt
1/2 teaspoon black pepper
Pinch of allspice

WHAT TO DO:

FOR THE SAUCE

Make the yogurt sauce by combining the yogurt, mint, lemon juice and garlic clove in a food processor. Pour the sauce into a container, refrigerate, and use as needed.

FOR THE BURGERS

1. In the same food processor, without washing it, pulse into a coarse paste the rosemary with the 2 cloves of garlic, parsley and onion. Add the rest of the spices.

2. Mix the rosemary paste with the ground lamb and shape into burgers. Refrigerate, until ready to use.

3. Grill the burgers, 3-4 minutes per side, on either an outdoor grill or in a hot, lightly oiled skillet.

4. Top each burger with yogurt sauce and serve as you would any other grilled burger. Or, serve the burgers do as we do—on a bed of mesclum between slices of gilled bread.

Green Herb Risotto

SERVINGS: Enough for 6

1 small onion
1 clove garlic
1 package of frozen spinach, thawed
1 bunch of fresh basil
1 bunch of Italian parsley
2 tablespoons butter
2 tablespoons olive oil
1 1/2 cups rice (Arborio is nice, but any other will do)
2 cups chicken broth
2 cups water
1/2 cup white wine
Salt to taste
1/4 cup Parmesan cheese, grated

WHAT TO DO:

1. Chop the onion and garlic in a food processor or by hand. Place in a small bowl and set aside.

2. In the same food processor (no need to wash it out), chop the spinach, basil and parsley. Set aside in another bowl.

3. Melt the butter in a saucepan and add the oil. When hot—before the butter starts to burn—add the onion and garlic. Sauté for a few minutes. Add the rice, stirring the whole time for an additional 5 minutes.

4. In a pitcher make a mixture of broth, water, and wine. Pour this, one cup at a time into the hot pot. Stir until the liquid is absorbed into the rice; add another cup and repeat the process until all the liquid is used up.

5. Stir in the chopped spinach, basil and parsley. Take the pot off the heat and cover. After 3 minutes, sprinkle with cheese and serve.

Glazed Carrots

SERVINGS: Enough for 4

1 pound carrots, peeled and sliced
2 tablespoon butter
1 tablespoon sugar
1 tablespoon vinegar
Salt and pepper
Fresh dill, chopped

WHAT TO DO:

1. Melt the butter in a skillet over medium heat.

2. Add the sliced carrots—in this preparation we like ours cut into thin, long diagonal slices.

3. Sauté for 5 minutes.

4. Stir in the sugar and vinegar and cook until carrots are tender and glazed. Stir frequently to keep from burning.

5. After about 10 minutes, check the carrots by eating one. Adjust seasoning as well as the need for any additional cooking time.

6. Serve, sprinkled with chopped dill.

Honey-Apricot Parfait

Our favorite apricots for this treat are the very short seasoned Blenheim type. Happily for us, Blenheims grow in our area and we have generous friends willing to share their bounty.

SERVINGS: Enough for 4

1 pound fresh apricots, pitted and cubed
3 tablespoons sugar
1 teaspoon lemon juice
2 cups Greek yogurt
Honey for drizzling
1 cup walnuts
1 tablespoon sugar

WHAT TO DO:

1. Toss apricots with sugar and lemon juice. Let rest in a bowl for up to one hour to heighten the flavor in the apricots.

2. Into a hot skillet, toss the walnuts with 1 tablespoon sugar and "toast" stirring constantly until sugar melts and coats the walnuts. Pour onto a cutting board and, when cool, chop coarsely.

3. Divide the apricots among your parfait glasses. Top with yogurt drizzled with honey and nuts.

COMFORT FOOD FAVORITES

Pork Tenderloin Roast

Veggie Sauce

Oven-Roasted Polenta

Blackberry & Ricotta Parfait

Our Favorite Snicker-Doodle Cookie

Pork Tenderloin Roast

SERVINGS: Enough for 4

One pork tenderloin
1 tablespoon soy sauce
1 tablespoon maple syrup or honey
1/2 teaspoon red pepper flakes, crushed
Salt and pepper
1-2 tablespoons Sesame Seeds

WHAT TO DO:

1. Preheat oven to 375 degrees.

2. Combine the soy sauce and honey in a small bowl, and brush the mixture all over the meat. Sprinkle lightly with salt, pepper, as well as some crushed red pepper flakes. Roll in a plate covered with sesame seeds.

3. Bake on a baking sheet for about 25 minutes. Transfer the tenderloin to a cutting board and, covered lightly with foil, let the meat rest for about a few minutes before cutting it into 1/2-inch-thick slices.

TIP: Pork tenderloin often comes packaged in twos. If that's what you have on hand, you might as well roast both pieces of meat at the same time and have some cooked pork on hand to include in any number of Chinese dishes.

Veggie Sauce

This hearty red sauce contains two secret vitamin-packed ingredients: Spinach and yams. And if you don't share that information with your kids, they just might insist that this is the sauce to cover all their future boiled pasta treats.

SERVINGS: Enough for 4

2 tablespoons oil, any type
1/2 cup onion, diced
1 clove garlic, minced
28-oz can tomatoes
1/4 teaspoon dried oregano
1/4 teaspoon black pepper
1/4 cup cooked spinach, either frozen or fresh
1/4 cup cooked yams or sweet potatoes, smashed
1 tablespoon molasses
1/3 cup Ricotta cheese

WHAT TO DO:

1. Heat oil in a saucepan and add the onion and garlic. Sauté until fragrant.

2. Add the tomatoes and spices and cook for another 20 minutes.

3. Take the pan off of the stove and stir in the spinach and potatoes. Blend the mixture with an immersion blender to make a smooth sauce.

4. Return the pot to the stove top. Stir in the molasses and cheese. When the sauce comes to a low simmer, serve.

TIP: As long as you're making the handful of smashed yams called for here, you might as well cook enough of this nutritious veggie and save it in the refrigerator as side dish for another meal. The same goes for the spinach.

Oven-Roasted Polenta

Polenta is just another name for cornmeal mush. But, with all the stirring called for in many recipes, it's rather a chore to make. Fortunately we have discovered an easier way: We bake it.

SERVINGS: Enough for 6

1 cup cornmeal (we like yellow for the color)
5 cups water
1 teaspoon salt
1 tablespoon olive oil
1 cup corn chips, crumbled

WHAT TO DO:

1. Preheat oven to 350 degrees.

2. Sprinkle cornmeal into a bowl with the water, stirring as you go. Add the salt and oil and pour out into a shallow baking dish.

3. Bake uninterrupted for 40 minutes. Stir and bake an additional 15 minutes.

4. Take out of the oven. Sprinkle with corn chips and let cool for 10 minutes before serving.

TIP: For cornmeal mush thick enough to cut up and fry in a skillet, cool overnight in the refrigerator.

Blackberry & Ricotta Parfait

SERVINGS: Enough for 6

2 cups blackberries
1/4 cup sugar
1 tablespoon lemon juice
1 1/2 cup Ricotta cheese
Sprinkling of nutmeg
Sprinkling of cinnamon

WHAT TO DO:

1. Reserving several berries for the topping, puree the rest with the sugar in a food processor until smooth.

2. To remove seeds: strain the berry mush into a bowl through a fine-mesh sieve. Stir in the lemon juice.

3. Sprinkle the Ricotta cheese with the spices and stir to mix.

4. In dessert cups, alternate layers of the blackberry puree with the Ricotta mixture. Finish with a whole berry on top, as well as a cookie for good measure.

TIP: To reach another level of goodness, slip between the layers either some chopped mangos or chopped peaches.

Our Favorite Snicker-Doodle Cookies

It might be the old-fashioned combination of cream of tartar and baking soda, or maybe it's the over-night rest in the refrigerator—whatever the secret, following this recipe exactly always gives us exceptionally good Snicker Doodles.

SERVINGS: 60 cookies

2 2/3 cups flour
2 teaspoons cream of tartar
1 teaspoon baking soda
1/2 teaspoon salt
1 cup unsalted butter, at room temperature
1 1/2 cup sugar
2 eggs
1 teaspoon cinnamon mixed with 2 tablespoons sugar

WHAT TO DO:

1. Combine with a fork the flour, cream of tartar, baking soda and salt.

2. In another bowl, beat the butter, sugar and eggs with an electric mixer until just smooth but not fluffy.

3. Add the flour mixture and stir until incorporated.

4. Gather the dough into a big patty. Wrap it in plastic and refrigerate at least one hour, or overnight.

5. When ready to bake the cookies, preheat the oven to 400 degrees. Form the dough into 1-inch balls. Roll them in the cinnamon sugar mixture and arrange about 2 inches apart on cookie sheets.

6. Bake for 15 minutes.

TIP: Like many cookies, both the Snicker-Doodle dough and the baked cookies freeze beautifully.

ALFRESCO EATS

Coconut Shrimp

Pineapple Salsa

Honey Sesame Chicken Wings

Romaine Leaves with Pasta Salad

Cornmeal Cake with Peaches & Cream

Party Ginger Tea

Coconut Shrimp

SERVINGS: Enough for 12

3 cups shredded unsweetened coconut
1/2 cup flour
1/4 cup cornstarch
2/3 cup ginger ale
1 teaspoon baking soda
1/2 teaspoon salt
1/2 teaspoon cayenne pepper
1 egg, lightly beaten
1 1/2 pounds large shrimp, peeled
Vegetable oil for frying
Fresh limes

WHAT TO DO:

1. Place the coconut in one bowl.

2. In another bowl mix the rest of the ingredients to make a light batter.

3. Dip the shrimp first in the batter, then coat with the coconut. At this point, the coconut-breaded shrimp can be kept in the refrigerator for up to one hour.

4. Heat oil to 350 degrees for frying.

5. Fry shrimp in small batches for about 5 minutes. Drain on paper towels.

6. Serve hot with a few drops of lime juice and accompanied with any fruity salsa.

Pineapple Salsa

1 pineapple, peeled, cored and diced
1 cup red onion, diced fine
1/2 cup cilantro, chopped fine
2 tablespoons jalapeno peppers, seeded and minced
Salt and pepper

WHAT TO DO:

1. Toss everything into a bowl.

2. Mix and let flavors develop at room temperature for one hour before serving.

Honey Sesame Chicken Wings

SERVINGS: Enough for 12

5 pounds chicken wings
1/2 cup soy sauce
1/4 cup rice vinegar
1/4 cup honey
2 tablespoons ginger, grated
2 tablespoons garlic, minced
2 tablespoons toasted sesame oil
1 cup green onions, sliced fine
1/4 cup sesame seeds

WHAT TO DO:

1. Combine the soy sauce, vinegar, honey, ginger, garlic and sesame oil.

2. Stir in the chicken and refrigerate overnight in zip-top bags.

3. Preheat oven to 350 degrees. Arrange on rimmed cookie sheets and bake for about one hour.

4. Before serving, sprinkle with green onions and sesame seeds.

TIP: For novelty's sakes, instead of sprinkling with green onions and sesame seeds, roll the wings in crushed Rice Krispies.

Romaine Leaves with Pasta Salad

SERVINGS: Enough for 12

1 1/2 pounds pasta (any small shape)
1 cup pesto sauce (either homemade or store bought)
1/4 cup Parmesan cheese, freshly grated
Black pepper, freshly grated
Head of romaine lettuce
Cherry tomatoes and basil leaves for decoration

WHAT TO DO:

1. Cook the pasta to taste, drain and rise in cold water.

2. Stir in the pesto.

3. Arrange lettuce leaves on a tray and fill each with the pasta salad.

4. Dust tops with cheese and pepper. Top with a couple of cherry tomatoes cut in half and add a fresh basil leaf.

TIP: The taste of store bought pesto can always be improved with the addition of a bit of freshly grated garlic as well as a spoonful of your best olive oil.

Cornmeal Cake with Peaches & Cream

You can bake this batter in a couple of loaf pans, but we like to use our favorite 10-inch-round Bundt cake pan.

SERVINGS: Enough for 12

1 cup butter, unsalted, at room temperature
1 cup sugar
6 eggs
1/2 teaspoon almond extract
1 cup flour
1/2 cup cornmeal
2 1/2 teaspoons baking powder
1/2 teaspoon salt
Confectioners' sugar, for dusting baked cake

WHAT TO DO:

1. Preheat oven to 350 degrees.

2. Stir with a fork, to blend the flour, cornmeal, baking powder and salt.

3. In another bowl, cream the butter with the sugar until light and fluffy, about 5 minutes.

4. Add the eggs, one at a time, beating thoroughly after each addition.
Stir in the almond extract. Fold in the flour mixture.

5. Pour the batter into a buttered and floured pan, and bake for about an hour.

6. When cool, dust with confectioners' sugar. Serve with fruit and cream.

Peaches & Cream

WHAT TO DO:

Peel and slice peaches into a bowl. Sprinkle with sugar and lemon juice and leave at room temperature for at least one hour. Serve with lightly sweetened whipped cream on the side.

Party Ginger Tea

SERVINGS: Makes about 12 cups

1 1/2 cups fresh ginger, peeled and coarsely chopped
5 cups boiling-hot water
1 tablespoon whole cloves
6 cups water at room temperature
1/2 cups fresh lemon juice
1 cup sugar

WHAT TO DO:

1. Mix the sugar with one cup of hot water in a saucepan and stir until sugar dissolves. Keep in refrigerator.

2. Using a blender, puree ginger with ½ cup hot water.

3. Stir in cloves and the remaining hot water.

4. Let the tea steep at room temperature for at least 2 hours.

5. Strain the steeped ginger tea through a fine strainer or some cheesecloth into a large clean bowl.

6. Stir in the sugar water and lemon juice. Pour into pitchers and refrigerate.

TIP: Drop a few thin slices of lemon into the pitcher for garnish.

Alfa

Soon after the birth of her 4th and youngest son, Alfa bundled up the baby and arrived in the sun filled courtyard of the Church of the Messiah. She enrolled in the Morning Garden program for moms and tots primarily to improve her English, she says. A neighbor had told her that an English-language component was part of the program. However, within a short time she realized that her fluency exceeded the rudimentary lessons offered. Still, Alfa kept coming for all the other doors the program opened up for her.

I'm always asking, searching for information. Good advice is often hard to find, you know. But at Morning Garden there are people that I admire: People who can show me how to educate myself, how to deal with my kids, how to save my marriage.

Now, bad advice is everywhere. It's all over the place. You have no idea how people you hardly know tell you to leave your husband. To spank your kids more. To do this. To do that. It's really a good thing that I believe in God and that I always ask him to guide me. Perhaps it was really God, even more than my friend, who brought me to Morning Garden? Maybe He brought us both?—Fernando and me.

As a mom, I'm learning so much about my baby's needs and my other bigger kids…. I'm figuring out that talking to them has often better results than spanking them. Not that I don't spank—you know, I do have four boys—sometimes my patience runs out. But I don't spank like my mom spanked us. She was so, how do you say, authoritative—is that a word? … I remember a lot of spanking. Now that I'm grown up, I can even understand her frustrations better than I used to. I remember her working all the time. There were seven of us children. And my dad used to drink a lot and beat her. I do suppose all that shaped her into a very, how should I say it, hard woman.

My husband never beats me. Perhaps he's just too tired? No, I'm just kidding. … The poor guy. For the third year now he's been working 3rd shift in a machine shop. When he gets home around 5 in the morning I try to give him a few hours of peace. I do what I can. I clear out the kids and he gets some sleep. But four hours just isn't enough.

Our place in not the best. It's what they call a studio apartment. That's an arty word for no room. Not only is there no room, there's way too much noise—and not just from our kids. There are the neighbors. They are not very considerate. The woman next door likes to play her music real loud. Not that I don't like music. … I like to dance a lot. My kids and I dance the salsa. I dance with my girlfriends at parties. … My husband? Oh, he's too shy to dance. … Probably he's just too sleepy, your right.

There's so much about my life I want to tell you, but my language is so bad. It's true that I'm always what do you call it a "chatter box." But I keep discovering that I'm missing so many words when I try to explain something. There are so many unspoken feelings inside of me.

I remember growing up in Mexico. I remember my childhood, how happy I was in our happy little town. My parents were very far away, working in Santa Ana. To tell you the truth, I never missed them. It is my grandpa that I miss, now. He was as my father, that's how I saw him. He always brought us mangos. He always gave us a little money.

My parents brought me to California from Puebla when I was fourteen. I remember it was winter, and it was so cold and scary. And I didn't speak any English. Those are not my happiest memories.

When I started school here, they didn't know where to put me: I was too old for middle school; I didn't belong in junior high either. But that's where I went. For the next four years I stayed in a Spanish as a second language curriculum. But I guess you'd have to call it Spanish as a first and second language, since there really was no other language.

Now I have started cosmetology school. A friend talked to me about this program, and now we're both in it. Its owner is Vietnamese. It costs me a hundred dollars per month. After eighteen months I will be a licensed cosmetologist. Right now I'm learning about bacteria, disinfectants, how to cut hair. All my classes are in English. I like that very much because that's helping me reach my dream to speak fluent English.

A happy woman is not someone who ends up domineering the lives of her children like my mother. She is now divorced from my dad and lives with my three younger brothers as their housekeeper, and she always complains. That's not how I want to end up.

I think a woman needs success in her own life. For me right now that would mean a better apartment—a place where my husband can get the sleep he needs. When I become a licensed cosmetologist, I plan to work and help financially so that my husband can get off the 3rd shift. I even see my kids going to college.

I don't want my kids to be like me. I want them to achieve more education. I also don't want my kids to become obese. Fat maybe?—but not obese. I'm afraid there's a lot of fat in the food we eat. But I'm doing better. Yesterday, I made tamales in a new way. With what?—with pork and some other *carnita*. But the new thing was that I put little pieces of squash in it. I never did that before. But that's a more healthy step, don't you think?

Maggie

At the age of thirteen, Maggie left the family home that her grandfather had built on a leafy street in Santa Ana and started her steady descent into ruin. By the time she was fourteen she had her first child, fathered by a 30-year-old neighborhood drug dealer with a raging temper: "I'll teach you not shame me," he repeatedly screamed at his doped up child bride; and Maggie, like clockwork, would end up at the local ER. When she was nineteen, he gave her a choice of either having the features of her face rearranged beyond recognition or all her teeth knocked out. She chose the knocked-out teeth. Teeth, no teeth, in and out of prison, made no difference to her, she recalls: "All I cared about was my next high. I used to be super irresponsible." That was then. Now, at the age of 33, Maggie has a job with the Department of Rehabilitation. She's the secretary of her neighborhood AA organization. She lives in a spotless two-bedroom apartment with her six-year-old daughter and--for the first time in her adult life --without a man. She's been drug free for three years.

Waking up sober is an awesome feeling. I used to wake up and immediately start worrying about how much alcohol or crystal meth I had to get me through the day.

It still amazes me when I think about how I've brought my life around from a cycle of drugs, assault and battery, prison, parole violation, possession, more violence, prison again.

My activity with drugs—all those wasted years—brought me nothing but pain. I was so tired of always losing and suffering. It was always the same. At Mercy House [a sobriety house, providing transitional housing for homeless women] and the Morning Garden program it's like I finally woke up and got a glimpse of living life from another perspective.

It was at Mercy House I became "the pride and joy of the program." And I don't want to let them down. Of course, I don't want to let myself down either, and I have a little girl to take care of. I don't want her to grow up on the street the way I did.

I learned to clean house. On Saturdays they would make us take everything out and "double scrub" our room. They taught me that cleaning was more than shoving my stuff under the bed and closing the door.

I budget my money now. I always have a little in savings left at the end of the month. I keep to the 10 o'clock curfew I learned there. I've disciplined myself in my eating and have lost 74 pounds.

I was shocked to see my body in a full-length mirror, when I got out [of jail] the last time. In prison they have these little shiny metal things just big enough to see your face in. I did notice the other girls putting on some pounds, but I didn't realize I was also becoming this really, really fat girl. You know there's not much to do there but fight and eat. And I worked in the kitchen and would also eat before and after each meal. In sixteen months I gained 80 pounds!

Why am I finally making the right choice? I don't know. Maybe it's because I didn't know anything and I was just too tired to keep going down the same old road. It's like I have now found a road map to success.

When my mom comes to visit my apartment, she sometimes brings my big kids with her. They all ask me, "Do you have a maid?"

My mom and dad got legal custody of my five older children. At the time, I didn't think their home was the best for them. My parents' alcoholic environment was not the best for me, I told the judge, but he said, "Alcohol is not a controlled substance."

Maybe the judge was right to award them custody. Maybe it was me that brought out the worst in my mom. Or maybe her temper brought out the worst in me. Most likely, the fault is mine because my sister, growing up in the same house, has always been perfect. She's had what I see now is called a normal life: She's never "used," she's got a job, she's getting married soon, she's got no addictions, no "priors," no kids. She's responsible. When I see my kids, they seem to be more like my sister than the way I used to be—angry, confused, lost to the world and myself.

Now that I have embraced structure in my life, I can see that I have a real chance of living a successful life. I want to be useful. I know I can reach out to others and pass along my experience to people who are misguided.

I do the orientation class for parolees getting out of prison. I met my own brother there. I see a lot of people who know me from the streets, from when I was active in the Gang. When they recognize me they always say, "Maggie, is that really you. You've changed so much! Where are your tattoos?"

The Gang? Yes, they do say that they'll come and get you if you leave. But that's just a myth. It's not like they're the Mafia. They're not that organized. A lot of them get deported back to Mexico. That's were the dad of my older kids is. I don't think he'll ever come back. He's 50 years old now, and I don't think he wants to be anywhere near here. He knows that this time he'll get 25 to life.

My little girl's dad was a bum too. I ran into him on the street a couple of years ago. He was asking me for money. I talked him into detox, and he's now manager of one of the Victory Outreach houses. He's even been paying me child support. It isn't much, but it's regular. He recently thanked me. That really felt good.

I feel like I have been reintroduced into society. I got my tattoos removed—on my face and neck. This one on my chest
is next to go: It's supposed to be a butterfly. "Not very good tattoo, is it?"

When I day dream, I think about how my life is improving. I can see myself as an accredited counselor. I see myself pushing my mom in a wheelchair, though, she's not in a wheelchair at all--I wonder what that means? I can see myself married to Gilbert [current boyfriend] and living together as a family.

I can see myself living with just my little girl and going to a nine-to-five job. I can even see myself in a place like Hawaii, where the water is so clean you see fish in it. That's about the only thing I remember about Hawaii. I used to take drugs there. But that was 10 years ago. And now I'm a different person.

To me, God is sobriety. I thank Him everyday for picking me out of the gutter and releasing me from the chains of addiction. Three years ago, an older lady in her eighties gave me this gold chain with a pendant of Jesus on the cross. I wear it around my neck everyday. It reminds me of my salvation from addiction.

Fall

apples

broccoli

brussels spouts

chile peppers

cranberries

dates

figs

nuts

oranges

persimmons

plums

pumpkins

sweet potatoes

yams

zucchini

AUTUMN MEAL

Pork Stew

Mashed Acorn Squash with Sage

Broccoli Crunch

Chocolate Silken Tofu Pudding

Lord Jesus be our holy guest,
Our morning joy, our evening rest.
And with our daily bread impart,
Thy loving peace to every heart.

Pork Stew

SERVINGS: Enough for 6

Oil for browning the meat
1 1/2 pounds pork shoulder, cut into 1-inch cubes
1 large onion, chopped
4 garlic cloves, minced
2 tablespoons fresh oregano or sage, chopped
1/2 cup white wine
1 1/2 cups chicken broth
2 tablespoons tomato paste
Pinch of allspice
Salt and pepper to taste

WHAT TO DO:

1. Pour enough oil to lightly coat the bottom of a heavy Dutch oven.

2. Add the pork, stirring occasionally until the meat is nicely browned on all sides—about 10 minutes. Transfer the pork into a bowl.

3. Add the onion and garlic to the Dutch oven and sauté until quite soft for about 10 minutes.

4. Stir in the oregano or sage, add the browned pork as well as the remaining ingredients.

5. Cover pot and simmer over medium heat for an additional hour.

TIP: If you have a handful of pomegranate seeds handy, sprinkle them on top of stew for a cheery presentation.

Acorn Squash Mash with Sage

SERVINGS: Enough for 6

3 heads of acorn squash, cut in half and seeded
1/2 cup sour cream
Salt and pepper
3 tablespoons fresh sage, chopped

WHAT TO DO:

1. Cut the squash halves into quarters. Place them in a pan and cover with water. Cook over high heat until just soft—about 10 minutes.

2. Drain the water out of the pot. Let the squash cool for about 15 minutes before removing the soft flesh from the skin with a spoon.

3. Run the cooked squash through a vegetable mill or mash it with a potato masher.

4. Stir in the sour cream, add salt and pepper, and reheat.

5. Before serving, quickly fry the sage in a bit of butter and sprinkle over the top of the mashed squash.

Broccoli Crunch

SERVINGS: Enough for 6

4 cups broccoli florets, including peeled and chopped stalks
2 crisp apples, sliced thin
1/2 red onion, sliced paper thin
1/4 cup shallots, sliced paper thin
1/4 cup candied walnuts

FOR THE DRESSING
1 garlic clove, minced
Pinch of salt
1/4 cup almond butter or peanut butter
3 tablespoons lemon juice
Pinch of brown sugar
2 tablespoons vegetable oil
2 tablespoons hot water

WHAT TO DO:

1. Bring a pot of water to boil. Toss in the broccoli, boiling the vegetable for just 30 seconds before pouring the contents of the pot into a colander. Drain the broccoli and immediately plunge into a bowl of ice water to stop further cooking. Once cold, take the broccoli out of the ice bath, allowing all the water to drain while you proceed with the recipe.

2. Make the dressing by processing the dressing ingredients either in a blender or with an immersion blender. Set aside.

3. Quickly fry the shallots in a bit of butter until golden browned. Set aside on a paper towel--they will crisp up as they cool.

4. Combine the cooked broccoli with the apples and red onions. Stir in the dressing. Sprinkle top with the browned shallots and candied walnuts.

Chocolate Silken Tofu Pudding

SERVINGS: Enough for 8

3/4 cup sugar
1 cup water
1 pound silken tofu
8 ounces semisweet chocolate, coarsely chopped
1 teaspoon vanilla
1 teaspoon cinnamon
Pinch of cayenne pepper
2 oranges, peeled and sectioned
Chocolate shavings

WHAT TO DO:

1. Combine the sugar with the water in a saucepan. Bring to a boil, stirring until the sugar dissolves.

2. Take the saucepan off of the stovetop. Add the chocolate, cover the pot, and set aside until the chocolate melts. Stir to combine the chocolate with the sugar water.

3. In a food processor blend until smooth the tofu, the melted chocolate, and seasonings.

4. Divide the chocolate tofu pudding among 8 small cups, and chill for 30 minutes. Serve garnished with orange sections and chocolate shavings.

TIP: Silken tofu (also called Japanese-style tofu) has the soft, creamy consistency required for success with this recipe. Though it's made from the same ingredients as regular tofu, silken tofu is processed differently and the two are usually not interchangeable.

WAY EASY TO MAKE LUNCH

Sausage and Pasta

Carrot Ribbons and Peas

Plum Pancake Baked in a Cake Pan

Sausage and Pasta

We always like to use Penne pasta for this recipe because it's readily available and it seems to be the right size. But that doesn't mean that any other bite-sized shape wouldn't be equally suitable.

SERVINGS: Enough for 8

1 cup onions, chopped fine
5 Italian sausages, sweet—not spicy
2 tablespoons fresh rosemary, chopped fine
2 bay leaves--crumbled
Hot pepper flakes to taste
1 can chopped tomatoes (28 ounces)
1 pound pasta
1 cup cream
1 cup Parmesan cheese, grated
Salt and pepper

WHAT TO DO:

1. After browning the sausage in a hot skillet, crumble it into a bowl.

2. Reheat the same skillet, unwashed, and sauté the onions. After 5 minutes, add the rosemary, bay leaves and hot pepper flakes, and sauté the mixture for an additional minute or two.

3. Add the browned sausage and canned tomatoes to the skillet, and simmer while the pasta cooks separately.

4. Cook pasta in plenty of hot water to desired tenderness, paying attention not to overcook. Drain the cooked pasta in a colander.

5. In the same pot used for cooking the pasta, heat the cream with a little salt and pepper. Stir in the sausage-tomato sauce and add the cooked pasta.

6. Serve on a large platter with a generous sprinkling of Parmesan cheese.

Carrot Ribbons and Peas

A combination of carrots and peas always makes a cheerful show on the plate. But sometimes, when we have extra hands on board, we shave the carrots with a potato peeler into ribbons just for some extra fun.

SERVINGS: Enough for 8

1 pound carrots
1 pound peas, frozen
3 tablespoons butter
1 teaspoon sugar
Pinch of salt

WHAT TO DO:

1. While bringing a pot of water to boil, peel the carrots and shave them into ribbons with a vegetable peeler.

2. Put the carrots into boiling water and cook. After 3 minutes of cooking, add the frozen peas and cook an additional minute or two. Pour the vegetables into a colander to drain.

3. Melt the butter in the microwave oven and stir it into the veggies.

4. Before serving, sprinkle with sugar and salt.

Plum Pancake Baked in a Cake Pan

Basically nothing more than fruit surrounded by a pancake batter, this fine recipe bakes into what the French would call a "clafouti." For tastiest results use prune plums, also called Italian plums.

SERVINGS: Enough for 6

FOR THE BASE
24 Italian plums, cut in half (north to south) and pitted
3 tablespoons sugar
2 tablespoons flour
1/4 teaspoon cinnamon
2 tablespoons candied ginger, chopped fine

FOR THE TOPPING
5 tablespoons sugar
3 eggs
3/4 cup heavy cream
3/4 cup milk
1/4 teaspoon ground ginger
1/4 teaspoon cinnamon
1/2 cup flour
Pinch of salt
1 teaspoon baking powder

WHAT TO DO:

1. Heat oven to 400 degrees.

2. Combine the pitted plums with the 3 tablespoons of sugar, 2 tablespoons of flour, and ½ teaspoon of cinnamon.

3. Arrange the plums in a close huddled spiral inside a buttered 9-inch cake pan.

4. Sprinkle top of plums with candied ginger.

5. In a food processor, combine the sugar for the topping with the eggs, cream, milk and spices. Blend until smooth.

6. Sift the flour, salt and baking powder over the mixture. Pulse until just blended.

7. Pour the batter over the arranged fruit and bake for about 45 minutes— until puffed and browned.

8. Cool, dust the top with powdered sugar, and serve either as is or with cinnamon ice cream.

WE LOVE SALMON A LOT

Asian Flavored Salmon Cakes
Couscous with Scallions
Roasted Veggies with Soy Sauce
Cinnamon Ice Cream
Sauted Apples

Couscous with Scallions

SERVINGS: Enough for 6

1 1/2 cup couscous
1 1/2 cup water
1/2 teaspoon salt
1 tablespoon olive oil
2 tablespoons scallions, sliced paper thin

WHAT TO DO:

1. Combine the couscous, water, and salt in a microwave safe dish, and cook in a microwave according to cooking directions on the package.

2. As you fluff up the cooked couscous, add in the oil. Sprinkle with the chopped scallions, and serve.

TIP: Because of its priciness, we're not the biggest fans of olive oil, but in this simple side dish it really does add another level of deliciousness. The scallions help too.

Asian Flavored Salmon Patties

SERVINGS: Enough for 6

1 pound fresh salmon, chopped fine
8 ounces ground pork
1 tablespoon butter
1/2 small onion, chopped fine
1 cup mashed potatoes
1 egg, beaten
Salt and pepper
Pinch of red pepper flakes
Oil for frying

FOR THE SOY DRESSING
1/4 cup soy sauce
1 tablespoon lemon juice
1 teaspoon chili paste
Pinch of sugar
1/4 cup cilantro, chopped fine

WHAT TO DO:

1. Make the dressing by whirling all the dressing ingredients with an immersion blender. Set aside at room temperature.

2. Melt the butter in a large skillet and sauté the onion until transparent. Set aside to cool.

3. In a large bowl combine the salmon with the pork. Add the rest of the ingredients along with the cooled onion, mix lightly and shape into 12 small patties.

4. Heat a slick of oil in a large frying pan and brown the salmon cakes evenly on both sides—about 3 minutes per side, (To ensure a perfectly delicious interior, resist the natural urge to press them down with the spatula.)

5. Serve with a dribbling of soy dressing or any other favorite sauce.

6. To make these moist salmon cakes even more juicy, we like to serve them either with our favorite soy dressing or with a mixture of mayonnaise and a dab of pesto.

TIP: These are also delicious made either with mashed sweet potatoes or any mashed squash.

Roasted Veggies with Soy Sauce

SERVINGS: Enough for 6

1 butternut squash, peeled and cubed
2 red bell peppers, seeded and diced
1 red onion, quartered
2 carrots, diced coarsely
2 parsnips, diced coarsely
Handful of fresh thyme
1 tablespoon fresh rosemary, chopped
1/4 cup oil
1 tablespoon balsamic vinegar
1 tablespoon soy sauce
Salt and pepper to taste

WHAT TO DO:

1. Preheat oven to 475 degrees.

2. Combine all the veggies, oil and herbs in a large bowl.

3. Line a rimmed cookie sheet with foil. Oil the foil and spread out the veggies. Sprinkle with salt and pepper.

4. Bake for 20 minutes.

5. Take the sheet out of the oven, sprinkle the veggies with the vinegar and soy sauce, stir and bake another 30 minutes, reducing the oven temperature to 400 degrees.

6. Before serving, pick off and discard the thyme stems. Stir once again.

Cinnamon Ice Cream with Sauted Apples

Since we frequently roll our unbaked cookie dough in cinnamon sugar, it was just a matter of time before we discovered how yummy this technique is on ice cream.

SERVINGS: Enough for 6

ICE CREAM

1 quart vanilla ice cream
1/4 cup sugar
1/2 teaspoon cinnamon

Using an ice cream scoop make 6 balls of ice cream and roll them in a mixture of sugar and cinnamon.

SAUTED APPLES

4-5 large apples
1 tablespoon butter
2 tablespoons brown sugar

WHAT TO DO:

1. Peel, core, and thinly slice the apples.

2. Melt the butter in a large skillet, add the apples, and sauté until they start to brown. At that point, stir in the sugar, and cook until the sugar dissolves into the apples.

3. Set aside to cool slightly. Serve warm with ice cream.

HEARTY LUNCH

Sublime Meatloaf Burgers with Gravy
Egg Noodles with Herbs
Caramel Apples on a Stick

Sublime Meatloaf Burgers with Gravy

Since we in Morning Garden like to make dishes that once cooked are easy to serve, we have discovered that pretty much any meatloaf recipe can be made into meatloaf burgers. We especially like this recipe--we think it's quite sublime.

SERVINGS: Enough for 6

1 1/4 pounds combination of ground beef, pork, and veal
Salt to taste
1 pound frozen spinach, chopped
1 clove garlic, minced
1 teaspoon pepper
1/4 teaspoon nutmeg
1/2 cup celery, chopped
1/2 cup onions, chopped
1/2 cup parsley, chopped
1 tablespoon butter
1 egg, beaten
6 slices of bacon
1/2 cup bread crumbs
Butter for browning the burgers

WHAT TO DO:

1. After microwaving the frozen spinach, place it in a colander to drain off any liquids.

2. In a food processor, chop parsley and set aside in a large bowl.

3. In the same processor bowl, chop onion, celery and garlic. Toss this into a hot skillet coated with melted butter and sauté for 3-5 minutes.

4. Squeeze most of the liquid out of the spinach and give it a few whirls in the food processor.

5. Combine the spinach with the chopped parsley in the bowl. Mix in the sauted onion, celery and garlic. Stir in the pepper, nutmeg and salt.

6. Add the meat and mix thoroughly, but with a light hand. Finally, stir in the egg.

7. Spread the bread crumbs on a cookie sheet, and make 6 burgers (or more, if you want them smaller). Wrap a slice of bacon around the edge of each burger, and bread each side with the bread crumbs. At this point, letting the burgers rest on whatever crumbs remain, put the tray in the refrigerator for one to three hours prior to proceeding with the recipe.

8. Preheat the oven to 350 degrees.

9. Melt 2 tablespoons of butter in a skillet and brown the breaded burgers for 3 minutes on each side. Arrange them side-by-side in a shallow baking dish and bake for 30 minuets.

TO MAKE THE GRAVY: Place 2 teaspoons of cornstarch into a measuring cup and slowly stir in 1 cup of chicken stock. Take burgers out of baking dish and, heating the pan up on the stove top, stir the chicken stock into the pan to combine with the drippings. Bring the gravy to a boil, add a pinch of salt and pepper, and pour over the burgers.

Caramel Apples on a Stick

SERVINGS: 16 small apples

1 pound dark brown sugar
1 cup butter
14-ounce can sweetened condensed milk
1 cup dark corn syrup
2 teaspoons vanilla
1/4 teaspoon salt
16 small Granny Smith apples
16 wooden chopsticks
Toffee bits
Melted chocolate
Paper cupcake liners
Instant read thermometer

WHAT TO DO:

1. Wash and towel dry the apples. Set them aside.

2. Combine first six ingredients in a heavy 2-quart saucepan and set it over low heat, stirring with a wooden spoon until the sugar dissolves.

3. Cook undisturbed for another 15 minutes, brushing down the sides of the pan with a brush dipped in water as a built up of sugar accumulates.

4. Increase the heat and cook the caramel at a rolling boil for an additional 10-12 minutes, all along stirring and occasionally, as needed, continuing with brushing down of the sides of the pan with the wet brush.

5. As soon as the caramel reaches 236 degrees on an instant-read thermometer, pour the contents of the pot into a metal bowl, and cool without stirring for about 15 minutes.

6. While the caramel cools to 200 degrees, line a baking sheet with aluminum foil sprayed lightly with vegetable oil. With a hammer tap a chopstick into the stem end of each apple.

7. Dip the apples into the caramel to coat. Arrange them on the cookie sheet for the caramel to set. Any caramel that pools along the base can be pressed back by hand just before rolling that part of the apple on a plate generously covered with toffee bits.

8. Melt the chocolate carefully in the microwave--it burn easily.

10. Scrape it into a plastic sandwich bag, cut off a small corner, and drizzle a few lines over each apple. Place the finished apples on pleated paper cupcake liners and serve.

TIP: If the caramel becomes too thick during the apple dipping process, whisk a tablespoon of whipping cream into the bowl and heat it over hot water until reaching the right consistency.

Egg Noodles with Herbs

SERVINGS: Enough for 6

1 pound dried egg noodles
Salt
Butter
Fresh herbs such as parsley, chervil, thyme—chopped fine

WHAT TO DO:

1. Bring a large pot of water to boil. Add some salt and all of the noodles at once. Stir and cover the pot with a lid or cookie sheet.

2. Take the pot off of the stove top, and let noodles steep in the hot water. In 20 minutes, when the noodles are done, strain them in a colander and rinse in cold running water to stop the cooking process. (At this point the noodles can be kept in the refrigerator for a couple of days to use as needed.)

3. When ready to serve: Melt some butter in a large skillet and stir in the cooked noodles. Sauté for a few minutes until hot. Finish off with a sprinkling of chopped herbs.

TIP: To have fresh herbs on hand, puree them with enough vegetable oil to make a thick paste to freeze in ice-cube trays. No ice-cube tray? No problem: Spread the mixture out on a plastic lined plate, freeze solid, slip the disk into a zip-top bag, and chip away as needed.

God is great and God is good,
Let us thank God for our food.
Amen

TRADITIONAL GRACE

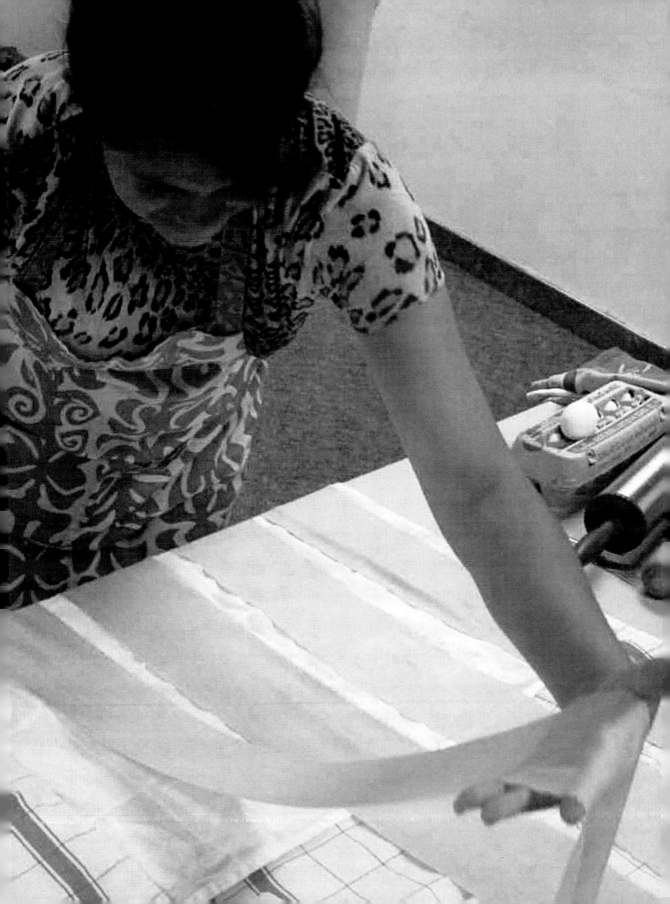

WE LOVE ITALIAN FOOD

Leftover Pot Roast Lasagna

Mixed Salad

with Cranberries, Walnuts & Oranges

Herbed Bread Sticks

Banana Pudding

with Berries & Cookies

Leftover Pot Roast Lasagna

Make the pot roast one day and have it for dinner—leaving enough for the lasagna. The next day, make the ragu sauce and serve some of it over a plate of fried hash browned potatoes. So, now that you have the leftover pot roast and the leftover sauce, all that remains is cooking the lasagna noodles and putting it all together.

SERVINGS: ENOUGH FOR 10

THE RAGU SAUCE
1 pound left-over pot roast, chopped
1 pound sweet Italian sausages
1 large onion, chopped
1 tablespoon garlic, chopped
Several sprigs of fresh thyme
1/2 cup red wine
Two 28-ounce cans tomatoes
Pinch of red pepper flakes

THE LASAGNA
2 pounds lasagna noodles, cooked and drained
6 cups ragu sauce (recipe above makes 12 cups)
3 cups Ricotta
1 pound fresh Mozzarella, shredded
1 cup Parmesan, grated
Fresh ground pepper

WHAT TO DO:

1. Brown the sausages in a large pot. Take out of the pot and, when cool enough to handle, chop into small pieces.

2. Into the fat rendered from the sausages, brown the onion. Stir in the garlic and red peppers flakes, followed by the sausage, chopped pot roast, wine and thyme.

3. Drain the liquid from the canned tomatoes into the pot. Add the tomatoes after first giving them a whirl in a food processor.

4. Bring the sauce to boil, reduce the heat and simmer for 3 hours.

5. Set the pot aside and cool the sauce to room temperature before proceeding with making the Lasagna.

6. Preheat oven to 350 degrees.

7. Using two 9x12-inch pans or one large one, oil the bottom of the pans and line them with a layer of cooked pasta, follow with several spoonfuls of ragu sauce and some scattered blobs of Ricotta, a sprinkling of Parmesan and ground pepper, and a small handful of Mozzarella. Repeat the layers twice, ending with Parmesan and Mozzarella on top.

8. Bake for 1 hour and 15 minutes. Let the lasagna rest out of the oven for at least 15 minutes before serving

Mixed Salad with Cranberries, Walnuts, and Oranges

We suggest that you mix fruit—any seasonal fruit will do—into your green salads in any amount to your taste. It never fails to impress.

FOR THE SALAD
Mixed salad greens
Dried cranberries
Walnuts, candied
Oranges, peeled and sliced thin

FOR THE DRESSING
1 cup oil
1/2 cup vinegar—any type on hand
1 tablespoon chopped onions
2 cloves of garlic
1 teaspoon Dijon mustard
Handful of fresh parsley
Salt and pepper

WHAT TO DO:

Blend the ingredients for the dressing with an immersion blender. Set aside to use for the salad. (Extra dressing will keep for weeks in the refrigerator.)

TIP: Use either store bought candied walnuts or make your own by simply tossing a handful of nuts about on a hot skillet along with a teaspoon or two of sugar. Watch carefully: They burn quickly!

Herbed Bread Crisps

Everyone really loves these. So you might as well make a lot. Any leftovers crisps you might end up with can be put through the food processor and turned into herbed bread crumbs, guaranteed to be better than any you could ever buy. But don't worry: There will be no leftovers!

1 baguette
Olive Oil
Salt
Red Pepper Flakes
Dried oregano
Sesame Seeds

WHAT TO DO:

1. Preheat oven to 350 degrees.

2. Cut the baguette on the bias into rather long ¼-inch-thick or thinner slices. You'll need a sharp serrated knife to do this properly.

3. Brush one side of each slice with some olive oil and sprinkle with the rest of the ingredients.

4. Bake until lightly browned—about 10 minutes.

Banana Pudding
with Berries and Cookies

SERVINGS: Enough for 6

Package of instant vanilla pudding
1 cup whipped cream
2 tablespoons brown sugar
2 bananas, sliced thin
Half of pint of berries, any
Cookie crumbs, any

WHAT TO DO:

1. Make pudding according to package directions.

2. Whip the cream with the sugar and fold into the pudding.

3. Layer parfait glasses with cream pudding, bananas and berries.

4. Finish with a layer of pudding, topped with cookie crumbs.

CREAMY, YUMMY LUNCH

Baked Chicken
with Cream Sauce
Mushroom & Rice Casserole
Nutella & Banana Cookies

Baked Chicken with Cream Sauce

SERVINGS: Enough for 6

3 pounds chicken thighs and drumsticks
Pinch of cayenne
1/4 cup flour
Salt and pepper
Butter

FOR THE SAUCE
1 tablespoon butter
1/4 cup onion, chopped fine
3 sprigs fresh thyme
2 bay leaves
1/2 cup white wine
1/2 cup chicken stock
1 cup crème fraîche
Salt and pepper
1 cup Gruyère or Swiss cheese, coarsely grated

WHAT TO DO:

1. Preheat the oven to 375 degrees.

2. Place the flour, cayenne, salt and pepper as well as the chicken in a bag and shake to coat the chicken evenly with the seasoned flour.

3. Arrange the chicken on a rimmed cookie sheet. Lay a thin pat of butter on each piece and bake for 30 minutes.

4. Meanwhile make the cream sauce by melting a tablespoon of butter in a saucepan. Add the onion and sauté for about 3 minutes, before adding the thyme springs and bay leaf and wine. Boil for another 3-5 minutes.

5. When half of the wine evaporates, stir in the chicken broth as well as the cream. Taste before seasoning with additional salt and pepper; strain out all the solids, and set aside.

6. After the chicken has been baking in the oven for half an hour, pour the sauce over the chicken, sprinkle with cheese, and bake for another 10 minutes, until the cheese melts.

7. Arrange the chicken on a platter. Sprinkle a few spoonfuls of sauce into the cookie sheet and stir to loosen the baked-on particles. Combine that with the rest of the sauce and pour it around the chicken. Keep warm.

TIP: Crème fraîche can be expensive to buy, but fortunately it's easily made at home by combining 1 cup whipping cream with 2 tablespoons buttermilk; cover bowl with a kitchen towel and let sit until thickened, up to 24 hours. Stir and refrigerate until ready to use.

Mushroom, Kale and Rice Casserole

SERVINGS: Enough for 8

8 ounces small brown mushrooms, quartered
1/2 cup onion, chopped
1/2 cup celery, chopped
1 pound kale, chopped
3 cloves garlic, finely chopped
4 cups cooked rice, any type on hand
1/2 cup chicken broth
1/2 cup cottage cheese
1/2 cup sour cream
2 eggs, lightly beaten
Salt and pepper to taste
Fresh thyme, chopped
1/3 cup Parmesan cheese, freshly grated

WHAT TO DO:

1. Preheat oven to 375 degrees. (You may bake this dish along with the chicken above.)

2. In a large bowl combine the rice, broth, cottage cheese, sour cream, eggs, salt and pepper, and thyme.

3. After several minutes of sautéing the mushrooms in a large skillet, oiled and piping hot, add them to the bowl of rice.

4. Reheat the same skillet, add a bit more oil and sauté the onions, celery and kale along with the garlic. After five minutes, combine these veggies with what's in the bowl.

5. Turn the mixture out into a buttered 9x13-inch baking dish. Cover with foil and bake for 20 minutes.

6 Remove foil, sprinkle the dish with the Parmesan cheese and bake an additional 20 minutes.

Nutella & Banana Cookies

SERVINGS: Makes 20 cookies

20 large round cookies, either home made or store bought
2 small bananas, sliced ¼-inch thick
1 orange
1/2 cup Nutella
20 raspberries
Honey or butterscotch sauce

WHAT TO DO:

1. Cut the orange in half and squeeze out the juice into a small bowl. Add the banana slices and stir gently to coat them in juice—this will keep them from turning brown. Arrange the slices on some paper toweling before placing them on the cookies.

2. Cover each cookie with a layer of Nutella. Follow with an arrangement of three banana slices. Dribble on some honey or butterscotch sauce and top with a raspberry.

That's it. You'll love it!

OUR THANKSGIVING TABLE

Turkey Roll-Up with Gravy

Kumquat-Cranberry Relish

Sweet Mashed Potato Bake

Pear and Gorgonzola Salad

Pumpkin Parfait

Turkey Breast Roll-Up with Gravy

If, like the rest of us, you're clueless when it comes to directions like, "cut the turkey breast diagonally so that it opens up like a hinged book, and pound it to an even thickness of 1/2 inch," ask the guy behind the meat counter to do this for you. It will make smooth sailing through the rest of this preparation.

SERVINGS: Enough for 10

1 turkey breast half (about 3 pounds) with skin attached, but boneless
and hinged like a book, pounded to an even thickness of ½ inch
1 tablespoon of vegetable oil

FOR THE STUFFING
2 tablespoons butter
8 ounces mushrooms, thinly sliced
¼ cup shallots, chopped fine
¼ cup celery, chopped fine
1 teaspoon sage, chopped fine
1 teaspoon thyme, chopped fine
2 tablespoons Italian parsley, chopped fine
Salt and pepper
½ cup chicken broth
1 cup white rice, cooked and cooled
1 cup wild rice, cooked and cooled
1 egg, lightly beaten
½ cup breadcrumbs
Salt and pepper

FOR THE GRAVY
½ cup white wine, not sweet
2 cups chicken broth
½ cup heavy cream
2 tablespoons butter

WHAT TO DO:

1. Melt the butter in a medium skillet. Add the mushrooms and sauté for a few minutes until they release their liquid and become quite soft.

2. Set the mushrooms aside in a large bowl. Reusing the same skillet, toss in the shallots and celery and sauté for a couple of minutes or so. Then, stir in the chopped herbs as well as the chicken broth and both the white and the wild rice.

3. Now, toss the stuff from the skillet into the bowl with the mushrooms. Add the egg and breadcrumbs. Mix well. This can be made up to two days ahead.

4. When ready to roast the turkey, spread the prepared turkey breast out to its full size (skin side down on the counter) and cover evenly with the stuffing, spreading it to within 1 inch of the edges.

5. Gently—so as not the squeeze out the stuffing--roll the turkey breast up, jelly-roll fashion, ending up with a compact cylinder encased in skin. Now you have what's in many cookbooks is called a "roulade."At this point it would be a good idea to refrigerate your turkey cylinder for up to 3 hours, because then the next step will be a lot easier to handle.

6. Tie the roulade at 2-inch intervals with butchers' twine, and season all over generously with salt and pepper.

7. Preheat the oven to 375 degrees.

8. Heat the tablespoon of oil in a small roasting pan on top of the stove, and brown the roulade on all sides.

9. Then, putting the roulade—seam side down in the pan, bake it uncovered for about 1 hour and 15 minutes. During the roasting time, brush a little melted butter on the roulade: the first time after 30 minutes and the second time 30 minutes later.

10. When an instant-read thermometer thrust into the center of the roulade registers 150 degrees—after about 1 ¼ hour, take the turkey out of the oven, place it on a platter, and cover it with aluminum foil for and an uninterrupted rest of 15 minutes. Meanwhile, make the gravy.

TO MAKE THE GRAVY:

1. Place the same roasting pan from the turkey on the stovetop, slowly stir in the wine and cook until all the browned bits from the pan are incorporated into the liquid.

2. At this point, add the chicken broth and cook for another 5 minutes.

3. If the thickness of the gravy does not meet your standards, this would be the time to add a mixture of 2 teaspoons of cornstarch with 2 tablespoons cold broth to the pan. Cook for an additional minute.

4. Reduce the heat, stir in the cream, whisk in the butter, sprinkle with salt and pepper. When the butter melts, remove the pan from the stovetop. Cover to keep warm.

To serve: Remove the twine from the roulade, slice it into 1-inch thick slices and pass the gravy.

Kumquat-Cranberry Relish

The kumquats in this recipe elevate the standard cranberry sauce to new heights.

SERVINGS: Makes about 4 cups

2 cups sugar
2 cups water
Pinch of ground cloves
1 cup fresh kumquats, sliced or quartered
1 pound fresh cranberries

WHAT TO DO:

1. Combine sugar, water and cloves in a large saucepan, stir in kumquats, bring to boil and cook for three to four minutes.

2. Add the cranberries and cook an additional five minutes until all the cranberries burst open and the sauce thickens.

3. Serve the relish as an accompaniment to any roasted bird dish.

TIP: No time to cook the sauce? No worry. Just add a handful of chopped kumquats to a can of cranberry sauce.

Sweet Potato Bake

SERVINGS: Enough for 6

FOR THE POTATOES
4 cups sweet potatoes, mashed
1/4 cup sugar
1/2 cup milk
3 eggs
1/4 cup butter, melted
Pinch of salt
Pinch of cayenne pepper

FOR THE TOPPING
1/4 cup cold butter
1/4 cup flour
1/2 cup brown sugar
1/2 cup pecans, chopped

WHAT TO DO:

1. Boil until soft 2-3 sweet potatoes to yield 4 cups of smashed potatoes. Combine these with the sugar, milk, eggs, butter and seasoning. Transfer to a greased 2-quart baking dish.

2. In a small bowl, combine the flour, sugar and butter using your fingers until you create a crumbly mixture. Sprinkle this over the potatoes, followed with the chopped nuts.

3. Bake uncovered at 325 degrees for about 45 minutes, keeping an eye on the nuts so that they don't burn.

TIP: The best way to "mash" the sweet potatoes is to force the cooked potatoes through a food mill. Second best is to mash them with either a masher or a fork. And that's about the only ways to do it: Don't even consider the food processor for this preparation.

Pumpkin Parfait

SERVINGS: Enough for 12

1/4 cup milk
1/4 cup sugar
1 tablespoon brandy
1 teaspoon cinnamon
1/2 teaspoon ginger
1/4 teaspoon nutmeg
1 pound pumpkin, canned
2 1/4 cups heavy cream
2 tablespoons sugar

WHAT TO DO:

1. Line an 8-inch square pan with plastic and put in the freezer.

2. Heat the milk with the sugar, brandy, and spice and cook until the sugar dissolves. Pour into a bowl and freeze for a few minutes just until cold.

3. Into the bowl from the freezer add the pumpkin and 1/4 cup of the cream. Mix thoroughly. Get the pan out of the freezer and pour in the pumpkin mixture. Wrap the whole pan in plastic and return to the freezer for at least 3 hours or overnight.

4. When ready to serve: Whip 2 cups of the remaining whipping cream with 2 tablespoons of sugar. Cut the frozen pumpkin mixture into cubes. Get out the parfait glasses and fill them with alternating layers of pumpking cubes and whipped cream.

TIP: A spoonful of kumquat-cranberry relish makes a cheerful red topping. Or sprinkle with pomegranates.

Morning Garden Comes to Your Table

GREAT ENCHILADA FIESTA

Pumpkin Enchilada Casserole

Poblano-Pepita Salsa

Apple-Cranberry Bars

Pumpkin Enchilada Casserole

Well worth making--especially when extra hands are on board to celebrate the glories of any leftover Thanksgiving turkey.

SERVINGS: Enough for 8

FOR THE SAUCE
10 dried California chiles
2 dried ancho chiles
6 garlic cloves
2 teaspoons oregano
1 tablespoon oil
1 tablespoon four
1 tablespoon brown sugar
1 teaspoon salt

FOR THE FILLING
2 tablespoons oil
1 onion, diced
4 garlic cloves, minced
1 tablespoon cumin seeds, crushed
3 cups pumpkin, peeled and diced
1/2 cup water
2 cups roast turkey, diced
Salt to taste

FOR THE ASSEMBLY
Oil
12 6-inch corn tortillas
3 cups Jack cheese, shredded

WHAT TO DO:

1. Stem, seed, and rinse the chiles for the sauce. Put them along with the garlic and oregano in a saucepan with 3 cups of water. Bring to boil and cook for 30 minutes. Pour chiles with cooking water into a steep-sided container, and blend the sauce smooth with an immersion blender. For the smoothest sauce: Force the through a strainer, and discard the solids.

2. Heat the oil in the same saucepan. Add the flour and stir for a couple of minutes. When the four and oil thickens, slowly pour in the strained sauce and bring to a boil. Stir in the sugar and salt. Keep warm.

3. For the filling, heat the oil in a skillet and add the onion. After about 10 minutes of cooking, stir in the minced garlic and crushed cumin seeds, followed with the diced pumpkin and water. Cook for 10 additional minutes. Add the turkey. Stir and season to taste.

4. Brush the tortillas with oil and, in a dry skillet, heat on both sides until pliable. Wrap in a tea towel to keep warm.

5. Preheat the oven to 350 degrees.

6. Spread 1/2 cup of sauce evenly into a 9x13-inch baking dish.

7. Arrange 4 of the tortillas (cutting them to fit as needed) over the sauce.

8. Spread a layer of sauce over the tortillas, followed by a layer of turkey filling. Cover the filling with 1 cup of cheese. Continue this layering sequence, ending up with the cheese layer, until everything is used up.

9. Bake for 30 minutes. Before serving out of the pan, allow for 10 minutes of cooling at room temperature.

Morning Garden Comes to Your Table

Poblano-Pepita Salsa

Any salsa that you might have left over, keeps nicely in the refrigerator for several days to use as an accompaniment to a plate of scrambled eggs along with any number of other dishes you can readily think of.

2 poblano chiles
1 pound tomatillos, husked and rinsed
1/2 cup hulled pepitas, roasted
1/4 cup cilantro, chopped
Salt

WHAT TO DO:

1. Char the chiles until blackened on all sides over a gas burner or on an outdoor grill (an electric stove top is not ideal for this step).

2. Place in a bowl covered with plastic. When cool enough to handle, peel, seed and chop finely. (To protect your hands from adverse reaction to the chiles, use plastic bags as gloves.)

3. Heat up a large skillet and sauté the tomatillos for 5-10 minutes. As they become covered with dark brown spots, take the tomatillos out of the pan. When cool, chop them coarsely.

4. In a food processor, pulse the pepitas with the cilantro. Combine with the chiles and tomatillos. Add salt to taste.

TIP: If time permits, the best thing to do to enhance the flavor of this salsa is to keep it at room temperature for up to two hours before serving.

Apple-Cranberry Bars

There are recipes for apple-pie bars galore, and there's also that seasonal favorite Cranberry Crisp; sometime it's just hard to decide which is best. So, we combined two recipes we had on hand and came up with this tasty winner.

SERVINGS: Makes 24 or more bars

FOR THE DOUGH
1 cup sugar
2 1/2 cups flour
1/2 cups almond meal
1/4 teaspoon salt
1 teaspoon baking powder
1 cup butter, diced in ½ cubes
1 egg

FOR THE FRUIT FILLING
2/3 cup sugar
1 tablespoon cornstarch
4 cups fresh cranberries
3 apples, peeled and sliced thin

FOR THE TOPPING
1/2 teaspoon cinnamon
1/4 of the dough

WHAT TO DO:

1. Preheat oven to 350 degrees

2. Mix the dry ingredients for the dough together in a food processor.

3. Add the butter and pulse a few times.

4. Add the eggs and give some additional pulses, until it all comes together.

5. Pat 3/4 of the dough into a 9x13-inch pan.

6. Combine the cranberries with the sugar and cornstarch.

7. Distribute evenly over the dough layer, cover with overlapping apple slices.

8. Into the remaining 1/4 of the dough, work in the cinnamon by hand to make a crumble. Sprinkle it over the fruit and bake for about an hour.

9. Cool slightly before cutting. Serve warm with ice cream.

Carla

Around the festive tables, a tot sits on every available knee. Center stage, sits a cake of *tres leches*. *Huevos Ranceros* headline the menu. The atmosphere in the activity room of the Morning Garden is humming with the celebration of Mother's Day. Our moms are telling us that in Latin America, the true intention of the day is not to shower mom with gifts but to honor the act of her motherhood with all the sacrifices that she has made for the wellbeing of her children. An internet rendition of Denise de Kalafe singing "Senora a su nombre es mi madre" emboldens the Spanish speaking part of the gathered celebrants to a tentative sing-along: *"...a ti me diste tu vida, tu amor, y tu espacio..."* [you gave me your life, your love, and your space]. Carla, tight lipped, swallowing hard, is trying with no success to keep her tears from flowing down her flushed cheeks.

I cry for this song: Now that I'm a mother, I miss my mom so much. I have not seen her for eleven years.

I grow up the baby of seven sisters. There are six brothers too. We live in Toluca, about 45 miles from Mexico City. When I was little, my mom always she go to work on the land and leave us alone.

When I have eight years, my older brother by two years was my best friend. The youngest brother, the baby of all the family, was born with Downs Syndrome, his mind never work right. When he starts talking, he doesn't know what to say.

The biggest surprise in my life was when I have 15; my parents give for me the celebration of my birthday. Never did I expect this because all my sisters never have the *quinceanera*. Everybody we know come to the party. Maybe 200 people? Everybody was invited. My big brother of 17 years bring seven of his friends from Mexico City. They make the music and I dance all day and all night, in my new *quinceanera* dress, with all the boys. They were so handsome. Everything was so beautiful.

The next year, when I have 16, I go to Mexico City to stay with my sister. When she was working, for four years, I only stay inside. And I feel very alone—like here.

I come here on a visa to work for a family from Guatemala. I take care of the kids and clean the house. When they leave for Miami, I stay in Santa Ana. My next job was in Santa Margarita. I get up at six every morning and take the bus for two hours one way and two hours coming back.

When I meet Jose and have a baby, I stop working. But to stay in the apartment everyday alone make me very sad. I have too much depression; one time I try to cut my hand. My stress was too strong. I go out on the street and didn't know where I was. My greatest fear is to be alone.

Now I don't feel so sad. I have four years when I go to the Christian Church [Pentecostal Church in Santa Ana]. Jose is more better too. Not perfect, but without so many problems like before. We get married, and now he have more commitment to our family. He is sensitive, more loving.

Me too, and I have more confidence to make things with my hands. I sew stuff for my church. In Morning Garden I learn how to cook more international. I like that very much. I like that I can learn English. I learn that it is my job to be responsible for myself, my kids, and my own family.

I hope for my girl [nine years old] that she will study more. I want for her to have a professional life. She is very intelligent. When I say something in English, she says, "Mommy, that's good. Now try to say it again. I help you pronounce." I think she will be a very good teacher. She will be the first teacher in our family.

My sister, she study in Mexico City. Now, she is a businesswoman. I think she has three, no, four fabric stores in Mexico. From my family she is the only one who has enough money to do what she wants. She has two kids. One is an architect.

I have many good ideas for business too, but I know that I need to learn more details about how to make and sell things. One reason why I want to learn very good English is to go to design school to study "couture." They have classes in Tustin. But they only teach the classes in English.

I wish my husband would try to speak more, but he doesn't want to improve his English. Like I say before, he is not perfect. His whole family has been here since before the '85 Amnesty. He is so lucky they are all here. I miss my mom everyday.

I don't even talk with my mom for eleven years because I can't call her. My sister in Mexico City, she tell me my mom's line doesn't work there anymore. They don't have a phone. The lines don't reach there, she say.

In Toluca, my family live on land for growing stuff. We have peach trees and many other fruits. But my favorite is the peaches from our garden. I hope someday to visit again and eat the peaches and to talk to my mom and to give her honor for that she is my mother.

I think it is possible to fix my papers when my girl is 21; the lady in immigration say, "maybe?" I think I still have time: My grandmother will have 100 years this year; my mom only have 71 years. In Mexico, we don't hurry. We always have time.

From my spiritual life I have happiness and faith that the bad things they get changed. I learn from my mom that with God in my heart and in my mind I will have a good life. "By yourself, you have nothing," she say. I hope it's true.

Shabano

Growing up in Pakistan, cosseted in a prosperous household headed by a government official, Shabano's only responsibility was to excel in school. Everything else in her life was handled by a covey of servants, cooks and drivers. Now, that type of existence is but a half forgotten dream and her Southern California days are filled with the responsibilities that come with raising a small child on public assistance. With no ready prospect in sight of ever bringing her economic standards above the basic level of survival, Shabano sees her goals distant and hard to achieve. "What gives me hope is that, at my core, I believe in the goodness that's within this country. I know that there are prospects that can be targeted; and, though the systems at times are very difficult to navigate through, I think that everything is intended for a good outcome," she says.

As harsh as my life has recently been, there are some measurable improvements: I started out homeless, moved on to a boarding house with lots of women and all the stress and domestic violence that came with their visiting husbands and boyfriends, and now I'm in an apartment that I share with just one single lady. Bethany and I finally have our own bathroom—for me, that's a big improvement in our lives and something to really be happy about again.

My happiest memories are not those of a life lived in Pakistan and Saudi Arabia without any material wants. Neither do my recollections of travel to France, England, even the Vatican make me as happy as remembering when our whole family lived together in Laguna Hills: Me, my mom, my dad, my two sisters, and my brother. My father was exploring his options of setting up a business and when things didn't work out with his partner, after three years, he was disappointed and the whole family returned to Pakistan. Except, I decided to stay here

I met my husband, through an introduction by friends, at Bally Total Fitness where I worked at the time. Soon I was expecting my baby, never imagining that Bethany and I would be homeless and living in a shelter provided by Catholic Worker.

Bethany was a name suggested to me by a pastor at Catholic Worker. I liked the sound of it—especially when combined with Theresa. Yes, it's quite different than mine: But now that I'm a Christian it seems quite suitable. My own name means princess. It's rather a common name in Pakistan, but I don't think it's a very suitable name for an American little girl.

Bethany is the light of my life. When I really think about it, she is the best thing in my life. Not only does she make me happy, I have a lot of fun with her. She is now taking ballet classes, every alternate Saturday. And it is such a great pleasure for me to see her blossom. I'm very privileged that Anaheim-Ballet has offered her a scholarship. She even has a very pretty outfit provided by her school.

Our days are very full. We catch the bus at 8:00 a.m. and don't get back before 6:30 p.m. When Bethany is at her school, I volunteer, assisting the teacher at the Literacy Center. After school, there are playground activities, as well as social skills lessons at Chalk Hospital. Also, in addition to her ballet lessons, she's learning to speak Spanish at the library. It is unfortunate that I cant help her with that language.

In our home we only spoke English. Because I am from Pakistan, people often presume that I speak Urdu. But I never learned a second language. In that regard, Bethany already surpasses me.

I'm very impressed that Bethany is so capable of maintaining a very full schedule. I think it's because she's been raised on programs. There was the infants and moms program with Catholic Worker; for three years we had perfect attendance at the Morning Garden program which I believe was instrumental in improving both our lives: Bethany learned how to maintain a schedule; I learned to set goals and not put the seeking of my own pleasure ahead of my child's wellbeing.

My biggest frustration in living here has been going through immigration. It seems that the obstacles to securing my fully legal residency here never end. There was the lengthy and arduous collaboration with the Pakistani embassy and a background check to make sure I'm not a terrorist or something otherwise illegal. Finally, when I was granted political asylum and got my work permit, I thought I would be set to work. Now that work authorization has expired, and I really don't know when I'll get my permanent green card.

A good job for me would be one that makes some use of my education. In Pakistan I finished my Masters degree which, by U.S. standards, has been downgraded to a Bachelor of Science business degree. Still that should be good for something I think.

I have at one time worked as a teacher in a charter school in Tracy, California—before changing my religion from Muslim to Christian, getting married, having a baby, being abandoned by people I trusted.

I'm very grateful to keep discovering how many good things surround even a bad situation. I think my Christian faith helps me in that regard. Also, the immigration judge told me to always seek "relief when you are helpless." It sounded like good advice, coming from a judge: I'm always trying to keep that in mind.

When I think about my past life in Pakistan, I really don't miss all the gold trinkets and the benefits of the maids, driver, and endless leisure that I had there. I just miss not living as a family. I think that when I have my own apartment, it will be like a dream come true.

Financial stability, a place of our own—not living as roommates with someone, living as a family with Bethany and my husband—if he chooses to live with us: That is something I hope and pray for. That would be my greatest treasure.

Winter

cabbage

citrus fruit

maple syrup

mushrooms, wild grown

mussels

pears

plantains

pomegranates

potatoes

root vegetables

rosemary

tangerines

turnips

Morning Garden Comes to Your Table

IN PRAISE OF COMFORT FOOD

Chicken Pot Pie with Biscuit Topping
Mango Roll-Up
Raspberry Sauce

Chicken Pot Pie with Biscuit Topping

SERVINGS: Enough for 6

FOR THE CHICKEN AND BROTH

1 whole chicken, cut into pieces
1 cup onions, chopped
1 cup celery, chopped
2 teaspoons dried thyme
2 whole cloves of garlic
Handful of parsley

FOR THE FILLING

1/4 cup butter
1/2 cup onions, chopped fine
3 stalks celery, chopped fine
1/4 cup flour
1 bag frozen peas
4 to 5 carrots, cubed
Mushrooms, quartered
Handful of fresh thyme or 1 teaspoon dry thyme

FOR THE BISCUIT TOPPING

2 1/2 cups flour
1 tablespoon baking powder
1 teaspoon salt
2 teaspoons sugar
2 cups heavy cream
2 tablespoons chives, minced

WHAT TO DO:

1. Place all the chicken pieces and broth ingredients into a stewing pot. Pour in enough water to cover the chicken. Bring to a boil. Cover the pot, reduce the heat, and simmer for a couple of hours. Take the chicken out and shred about half of it, reserving the rest for another recipe. Strain the chicken broth to make 5 cups.

2. Melt the butter in a large saucepan. Add the onions and celery. Cover and cook until the onion is transparent and the celery is soft. Sprinkle in the flour. Stir until the flour starts to "color." Now, slowly add the chicken broth, stirring constantly. When the sauce thickens, add the shredded chicken and the remaining filling ingredients. Pour this mixture into a buttered casserole dish.

3. Preheat oven to 375 degrees.

4. Stir together the flour, baking powder, and sugar in a bowl. Add the cream and chives. Stir just enough until the dough holds together. Drop heaping 1/4 cupful of the batter on top of the casserole dish. Bake until the biscuit tops turn a pale gold--about 30 minutes. Serve out of the casserole.

Mango Roll-Up

SERVINGS: Enough for 8

FOR THE CAKE
4 eggs, separated into yolks and whites
1 teaspoon vanilla extract
1/2 cup sugar, divided
Pinch of salt
3/4 cup flour

FOR THE FILLING
1 cup heavy whipping cream
2 tablespoons sugar
1/2 teaspoon fresh ginger, grated fine
2 mangos, chopped fine

FOR THE FINISHING
1 mango, cubed
1/2 cup raspberries
Powdered sugar for dusting

WHAT TO DO:

1. Butter a shallow 15 x 10-inch baking pan. Line the pan with parchment paper. Butter the paper and dust with flour. Preheat the over to 350 degrees.

2. Beat the whipping cream into soft peaks. Towards the end of the beating, add the sugar a spoonful at a time. Stir in the ginger and mangos. Cover and set aside in the refrigerator.

3. Beat the egg yolks for a couple of minutes, gradually adding 1/4 cup of the sugar. Beat until the mixture is thick and pale-colored. Sprinkle with the flour and quickly combine with a light hand.

4. In another bowl, beat the egg whites with a pinch of salt for couple of minutes until they are stiff. Towards the end of the beating process, add the remaining 1/4 cup of sugar. Gently fold the egg yolk mixture into the beaten egg whites.

5. Spread the batter evenly into the prepared pan. Bake about 12 minutes. Remove the cake from the pan onto a clean dish towel. Cool, covered with another dish towel to keep the cake from drying out.

6. When the cake is completely cool, cover its surface with the filling. With the help of the dish towel on the bottom as a guide, roll the cake up into a cylinder. Place the cake log, seam side down, on a serving plate.

7. Cover the log with a dusting of powdered sugar.

8. Serve with additional mangos and raspberries on the side. Pass the raspberry sauce around.

Raspberry Sauce

SERVINGS: Makes about one cup

1/2 pint of raspberries
2 tablespoons sugar
A few drops of lemon juice

WHAT TO DO:

1. Puree the fruit with the sugar in a food processor or with an immersion blender. Stain the seeds out of the sauce.

2. Taste and add a few drops of lemon juice to liven up the flavor.

KID-FRIENDLY MUNCHING

Tortilla Rollups
Avocado Dip with Salsa & Ketchup
Enormously Tasty Tomato Soup
Blueberry, Mango, Banana Pudding

Tortilla Rollups

1 cup cooked or roasted chicken, chopped fine
1/2 cup Jack cheese, shredded
1 cup canned pumpkin puree or sweet potatoes
4 ounces cream cheese
Salt and pepper
6 burrito-size tortillas, cut in half

WHAT TO DO:

1. Preheat the oven to 350 degrees. Line a cookie sheet with foil.

2. In a bowl, stir the cream cheese with the pumpkin puree until well combined. Add the rest of the ingredients, except for the tortillas.

3. Spread about 2 tablespoons of filling along the straight edge of a tortilla half and roll up into a "cigar." Repeat with the remaining tortillas.

4. Place the rolls seam-side down on the cookie sheet. Bake 5 to 7 minutes.

Avocado Dip with Salsa & Ketchup

SERVINGS: Makes 1½ cups

2 avocados, mashed with fork
1/2 cup yogurt
1 clove garlic, minced
Pinch of salt
1/4 cup tomato salsa, drained and pureed
1/4 cup ketchup

WHAT TO DO:

1. Combine the mashed avocados with the yogurt.

2. Add the garlic mixture and mix well.

3. Stir the drained, pureed salsa with the ketchup.

Serve as a dip for the tortilla wraps.

Enormously Tasty Tomato Soup

SERVINGS: Enough for 8

4 cans (28 ounces each) whole tomatoes
2 tablespoons brown sugar
1 large onion, minced
1/4 cup tomato paste
1/4 teaspoon allspice
2 tablespoons butter
2 tablespoons flour
3 cups chicken stock
1 cup whipping cream
1 tablespoon balsamic vinegar
Cayenne pepper
Salt

WHAT TO DO:

1. Drain the tomatoes in a colander over a bowl, reserving the liquid. Line a large rimmed cookie sheet with foil. Preheat the oven to 450 degrees.

2. Spread the tomatoes on the cookie sheet over the foil. Sprinkle with brown sugar. Bake for 30 minutes.

3. Melt butter in a saucepan. Add the onions and cook covered until the onions are softened. Add the flour, and stir the paste constantly for about a minute to create a roux. Add the tomato paste and allspice to the roux.

4. In a large soup pot, combine the roasted tomatoes with the roux mixture. Puree with an immersion blender until smooth. Slowly stir in the chicken stock and reserved tomato juice. Bring to a boil and simmer for 30 minutes.

5. Finish off by stirring in the cream and vinegar. Season to taste with cayenne pepper and salt.

Layered Blueberry, Mango, Banana Pudding

SERVINGS: Enough for 6

3-ounce package instant vanilla pudding mix
2 cups milk
3 bananas, mashed
1 cup heavy whipping cream
1 tablespoon sugar
1 mango, sliced thinly
1 cup blueberries

WHAT TO DO:

1. Mash the bananas. Thinly slice the mango ribbon thin.

2. Prepare the instant pudding according to the directions on the box. Add the mashed bananas and combine gently.

3. Whip the cream with the sugar into soft peaks.

4. Spoon the banana-pudding mixture into the serving cups, leaving room for the toppings. Place a layer of whipped cream on the pudding, top with the blueberries and mango slices.

WINTER SOLSTICE MEAL

Double Corn Muffins

Bean and Pasta Soup

Lemon Mousse with Berries

Double Corn Muffins

SERVINGS: 12 Muffins

Butter, soft, for coating muffin pan
1 1/4 cups flour
3/4 cup stone-ground yellow cornmeal
1 tablespoon baking powder
1/4 teaspoon salt
8 tablespoons (1 stick) butter, chilled and cut into ½-inch cubes
1/2 cup sugar
2 large eggs, at room temperature
1/4 cup whole milk
7-ounce can of corn, drained

WHAT TO DO:

1. Preheat the oven to 400 degrees. Brush the insides of the muffin cups with the softened butter, also lightly coating the top of the pan.

2. In a medium bowl, whisk together the flour, cornmeal, baking powder, and salt. Set aside.

3. In a large bowl, beat the butter and sugar with an electric mixer on high speed until the mixture is very light in color and texture, about 5 minutes.

4. Add the eggs one at a time, beating well after each addition.

5. Reduce the speed to low. Starting with 1/3 of the flour mixture, beat it into the butter and sugar mixture. Follow with 1/2 of the milk and mix again. Repeat with the next 1/3 of the flour, followed by the last half of the milk. Finish with the last 1/3 of the flour mixture. Stir in the canned corn.

6. Using a 2 1/2-inch-diameter ice-cream scoop, portion the batter into the muffin cups.

7. Bake for 10 minutes. Reduce the oven to 375 degrees and continue baking until the tops of the muffins are golden brown and a toothpick inserted into the center of a muffin comes out clean, about 15 minutes.

8. Cool in the pan for 10 minutes. Remove the muffins from the pan and cool completely.

Bean and Pasta Soup

SERVINGS: Enough for 8

1/4 pound bacon or Pancetta
1 onion, chopped
2 carrots, chopped
1 stalks celery, chopped
2 cloves garlic, minced
8 cups chicken stock
1 pound of dried beans, cooked
1 sprig fresh rosemary, chopped fine
1 cup small pasta shapes
2 tablespoons tomato paste
Salt and pepper to taste
Fresh grated Parmesan cheese for serving

WHAT TO DO:

1. In a soup pot, brown the bacon—about 5 minutes.

2. Add the veggies and stir-fry for an additional 5 minutes. Stir in the garlic and rosemary, and cook until fragrant—no more than 1 minute.

3. Add the beans along with the chicken stock and pasta, bring to a boil and, reducing the heat, cook for 30 minutes.

4. Stir in the tomato paste. Add salt and fresh ground pepper.
Serve in heated bowls, passing the Parmesan cheese around.

TIP: To save time, do like we do and use canned beans. Just remember that the soup will taste better and fresher if you drain the liquids and rinse the beans with fresh water before adding them to the pot.

Lemon Mousse with Berries

SERVINGS: Enough for 6

2 cups whipping cream
1/4 cup sugar
1 cup lemon curd, store bought
2 cups blueberries
Mint leaves for garnish

WHAT TO DO:

1. With a mixer or hand-held whisk, whip the cream into soft peaks, adding the sugar by spoonfuls towards the end of the whipping process.

2. Combine the whipped cream, thoroughly but gently, with the lemon curd.

3. Fill small, clear-glass, dessert cups half full. Sprinkle a layer of blueberries, followed by another layer of the lemon mousse.

4. Decorate the tops with several blueberries and a mint leaf.

HAPPY CHINESE NEW YEAR CHOW

Asian Beef Tacos

Asian Pork Tacos

Napa-Romaine Slaw

Kimchi Fried Rice

Almond-Coconut Cookies

Fruit Salad on a Stick

Fresh Ginger Soda

Asian Beef Tacos

SERVINGS: 18 tacos

1 1/2 pounds beef rib eye, thinly sliced
2 tablespoons soy sauce
1/4 cup sugar
3 to 4 garlic cloves, minced
2 teaspoons sesame oil
2 teaspoons mirin
2 teaspoons water
18 tortillas

WHAT TO DO:

1. Combine all ingredients and marinate at least 2 hours or up to 24 hours.

2. Cook meat on a grill or in a skillet.

3. Chop the meat to make the taco filling.

4. Fill the warmed tortillas with the beef along with a spoonful each of the kimchi rice (see recipe on page 159) and the napa-romaine slaw (see recipe on page 158).

5. Fold in half and serve.

TIP: For this recipe we buy our meat already sliced paper thin, available at any Asian market.

Asian Pork Tacos

SERVINGS: Enough for 12 tacos

1 pound pork shoulder, thinly sliced
3 tablespoons coarse-ground hot Korean red pepper powder
1 tablespoon soy sauce
1 tablespoon sugar
1 tablespoon sesame oil
3 to 4 garlic cloves, minced
2 tablespoons mirin (Japanese sweet wine)
Pinch of black pepper

WHAT TO DO:

1. Combine all ingredients and marinate at least 2 hours or up to 24 hours.

2. Cook meat on a grill or in a skillet.

3. Chop the meat to make the taco filling.

4. Fill warmed tortillas with the pork along with a spoonful of kimchi rice and napa-romaine slaw each.

3. Fold in half and serve.

TIP: As with the beef, we buy the thinly sliced pork at an Asian market. Look for it in the frozen meat section.

Napa-Romaine Slaw

SERVINGS: Enough for 6

FOR THE SALAD

4 cups (5 ounces) romaine lettuce, shredded
2 cups (3 ounces) Napa cabbage, shredded
1/2 cup (2 ounces) onion, sliced paper thin
Toasted sesame seeds

FOR THE DRESSING

1 tablespoon soy sauce
1 1/2 teaspoons lime juice
1 1/2 teaspoons toasted sesame oil
1/4 teaspoon sugar

WHAT TO DO:

1. Whisk together all the dressing ingredients. Set aside.

2. In a large serving bowl, combine the dressing with the romaine, cabbage, and onions.

3. Add more dressing to taste and garnish with the sesame seeds.

Kimchi Fried Rice

SERVINGS: Enough for 4

4 cups cooked white rice, chilled
4 strips bacon, cut into ½-inch pieces
2 cups store bought cabbage kimchi, diced
1 tablespoon butter
2 teaspoons sesame oil
Salt to taste
Sesame seeds
Green onions, sliced thin—both green and white parts

WHAT TO DO:

1. Over medium heat sauté the bacon in a large skillet or wok. Add the kimchi and cook several additional minutes.

2. Increase the heat to high. Add the rice and stir fry for several minutes, until the rice begins to brown.

3. Stir in the butter and sesame oil. Adjust the seasoning with salt.

4. Garnish with the sesame seeds and green onions.

Morning Garden Almond-Coconut Cookies

SERVINGS: Makes 3 dozen cookies

1 cup shortening
1 1/2 cup sugar
1 egg
1 tablespoon water
1 teaspoon almond extract
2 1/2 cups flour
1 teaspoon baking powder
1/2 teaspoon baking soda
1/2 cup sweetened, shredded coconut
Whole almonds for top of cookies

WHAT TO DO:

1. Preheat the oven to 375 degrees. Cream the sugar with the shortening. Add the egg, water, and almond extract. Beat until fluffy for another minute.

2. Sift the flour with the baking soda and powder. Combine with the beaten sugar mixture. Finally, stir in the coconut.

3. Shape the dough into small balls by rolling them between the palms of your hands. Arrange the balls on a parchment-lined cookie sheet. Coat the bottom of a drinking glass with butter and sugar, and use the glass to lightly flatten the cookie balls, replenishing the bottom of the glass with sugar as needed.

4. Place an almond in the center of each cookie. Bake up to 15 minutes.

TIP: This is a little like gilding the lily, but if you brush a little beaten egg white on top of the unbaked cookies, they will come out the oven with a little sheen.

Fruit Salad on a Stick

Mandarin oranges
Bananas
Orange juice
Pineapple
Mini marshmallows
Bamboo skewers

WHAT TO DO:

Remove grapes from stems. Section the Mandarin oranges. Cut the bananas into chunks and dip in orange juice. Cut pineapple into chunks.
Thread the fruit onto bamboo skewers. Top each point of the skewer off with a marshmallow.

Fresh Ginger Soda

SERVINGS: Enough for 6-8 drinks

1 ½ cup ginger, peeled and chopped in food processor
1 ½ cup sugar
1 ½ cup lemon juice, freshly squeezed
2-liter bottle of club soda

WHAT TO DO:

1. Combine the ginger, sugar, and lemon juice in a saucepan. Bring to boil. Stir to dissolve the sugar, and set aside to cool.

2. When cooled to room temperature, strain through a fine meshed sieve into a jar, and refrigerate to use as needed.

3. To serve, pour 3-4 tablespoons of ginger juice into a tall glass. Fill to the top with club soda, stir and serve with a colorful straw.

Morning Garden Comes to Your Table

LOVE IS IN THE AIR

Spicy Baked Chicken

Cobb Potato Salad

Pecan Tarts

Spicy Baked Chicken

SERVINGS: Enough for 4

4 chicken legs
1/4 cup sugar
1/4 cup salt
1 cup hot water, plus cold water
2 tablespoons butter
1 tablespoon Dijon mustard
Hot pepper flakes to taste
2 cups fresh bread crumbs
Salt to taste

WHAT TO DO:

1. Combine the sugar, salt, and hot water, and stir until dissolved. Add cold water to make 1 quart of liquid. Now you have what's called a brine. Place the chicken in the brine, cover, and refrigerate several hours or overnight.

2. Preheat the oven to 350 degrees.

3. Melt the butter and combine it in a bowl with the mustard and hot pepper flakes. Place the bread crumbs and salt in another shallow bowl.

4. Take the chicken pieces out of the brine and dry them with paper towels. Then, dip them first in the butter mixture, and roll them in the bread-crumb mixture.

5. Arrange the chicken, without crowding the pieces, in a shallow baking pan. Bake for 40 to 45 minutes.

TIP: It has been our experience that whenever we have enough time and foresight to brine any pieces of meat appearing on our menus, everyone raves about the tenderness, the moisture, the deliciousness of the dish. Therefore, we highly recommend this step—especially when dealing with chicken and pork.

Cobb Potato Salad

FOR THE SALAD

8 Russet potatoes
1/4 pound bacon, chopped
2 thyme sprigs
1 red onion, chopped fine
Salt and pepper to taste
4 tomatoes, cubed
4 avocados, cubed
¼ cup blue cheese, crumbled
1 packaged of any salad greens
1 tablespoon Dijon mustard

FOR THE DRESSING

2/3 cup oil (2 parts)
1/3 cup vinegar (1 part)
2 garlic cloves, minced
2 tablespoons parsley, minced
1 teaspoon salt

WHAT TO DO:

1. Boil the potatoes in their skins until tender. Slip the potatoes out of their skins and slice them thinly. Set aside in a large mixing bowl.
2. Sauté the bacon along with the thyme. When the bacon is browned and all the leaves fall off the thyme sprigs, take the bacon out of the skillet and set aside the cool.
3. Make the salad dressing in a steep-sided bowl or jar by blending all the ingredients with an immersion blender.
4. Into the bowl of potatoes toss the onions and pour in about half of the salad dressing. Mix the potato salad gently and mound it in the center or a large, shallow serving dish. Mix the salad greens with some of the remaining dressing, and arrange around the potato salad.
5. On top of the potatoes, alternate strips of avocados with tomatoes. Sprinkle with a few spoonfuls of salad dressing.
6. Combine the fried bacon and thyme and with the crumbled blue cheese. Sprinkle over the salad greens.

Pecan Tarts

The only thing that might be a little out of the ordinary in this recipe is your access to two of those mini-muffin pans. But once you have those, you'll be delighted with how simple as well as delicious this little tart is.

SERVINGS: 48 mini tarts, at least

FOR THE PASTRY

6 ounces cream cheese
1 cup butter
2 cups flour

FOR THE FILLING

2 eggs
1 1/2 cups brown sugar
2 tablespoon butter
2 teaspoon vanilla
1 1/4 cup pecans, chopped fine

FOR THE TOPPING

Pecan halves

WHAT TO DO:

1. Blend all pastry ingredients in a mixer. Form the mixture into a ball. Cover with plastic wrap and chill.

2. Whisk all of the filling ingredients together in a bowl and set aside. Preheat oven to 350 degrees.

3. With the palms of your hands roll the pastry dough into teaspoon-size balls. Place the dough balls into a nonstick mini-muffin pan. Using your thumb and finger, press the dough balls evenly into bottoms and up the sides.

4. Pour the filling into the formed tarts. Top each one with a pecan half. Bake until the filling is set, about 30 minutes.

MUCHO DELICIOSO
ON ALL COUNTS

Chicken and Ketchup

Longevity Noodles and Veggies

Coconut Cupcakes

with Cream Cheese Icing

Chicken and Ketchup

SERVINGS: Enough for 6

1 1/2 pounds boneless chicken thighs, chopped into 1-inch chunks
1/2 cup flour
1 tablespoon corn starch
6 tablespoons canola or corn oil
Salt and pepper
2 tablespoons garlic, slivered
1/4 teaspoon cayenne pepper, or to taste
1 cup ketchup

WHAT TO DO:

1. Combine the flour, cornstarch, and salt and pepper.

2. Dust the chicken with the flour and cornstarch mixture.

3. Put 2 tablespoons of oil in a large skillet, and turn the heat to high. Add just enough of the chicken pieces to form one layer.

4. When the chicken browns on one side, turn it over and brown the other side. Altogether, this step shouldn't exceed 10 minutes. Once fried, remove the chicken to a plate, and brown any remaining chicken pieces. Turn off the heat and let the skillet cool for a moment.

5. Add 2 tablespoons of oil to the skillet and turn the heat to medium high. Add the garlic and cayenne pepper and cook, stirring, about 2 minutes. Add ketchup and stir; cook until ketchup bubbles and darkens slightly.

6. Return the chicken to the skillet and stir to coat with the sauce. Taste and adjust seasonings. Serve with Spaghetti or Longevity noodles (recipe on following page).

Longevity Noodles and Veggies

SERVINGS: Enough for 6

12 ounces thin fresh noodles, like lo mein or tagliarini
2 teaspoons toasted sesame oil
3 cups Napa cabbage, thinly sliced
2 cups fresh shitake mushrooms (about 4 ounces), thinly sliced
4 green onions, chopped fine
2 tablespoons toasted sesame seeds
2 tablespoons soy sauce

WHAT TO DO:

1. Bring a medium saucepan of water to a boil over high heat and cook noodles until just done, 3 to 5 minutes, stirring to prevent sticking. Drain in a colander and rinse with cold water, then shake well to remove water. Sprinkle with the sesame oil and set aside.

2. In a large skillet, heat 1 tablespoon of oil. Add the cabbage and mushrooms and stir-fry for 1 minute until just wilted but not cooked. Add the noodles and stir-fry 30 seconds, moving constantly to heat through. Place in the bowl, sprinkle with the green onions and sesame seeds, drizzle the soy sauce on top and serve.

Coconut Cupcakes
with Cream Cheese Icing

Make cupcakes from a mix according to package directions, adding a teaspoon of coconut extract to the batter.

FOR THE ICING

1/2 cup sweetened dried coconut flakes
6 ounces cream cheese, at room temperature
4 tablespoons butter, at room temperature
2 teaspoons lemon juice
1/2 teaspoon vanilla
3 cups confectioners' sugar, sifted

WHAT TO DO:

1. Spread the coconut on a baking sheet and bake at 350 degrees until lightly toasted—about 10 minutes. Set aside to cool.

2. Beat together by hand the cream cheese, butter, lemon juice, and vanilla. Gradually add the confectioners' sugar, beating until the icing is smooth.

3. Spread the icing on the cooled cupcakes. Sprinkle tops with the toasted coconut.

ST. PAT WOULD EAT THIS

Potato and Fish Bake

Green Beans with Hazelnuts

Apricot-Kissed Apple Pie

Potato and Fish Bake

SERVINGS: Enough for 6

1 1/4 pound medium-size potatoes
1/4 cup oil, divided
1 tablespoon fresh thyme leaves, divided
Salt and pepper to taste
2 pounds firm, white, skinned fish fillets
1 cup fresh bread crumbs or panko
1 clove garlic, minced
1 cup cream
2 tablespoons parsley, minced
1 lemon, cut into wedges
Ketchup

WHAT TO DO:

1. Preheat oven to 400 degrees. Wash and cut potatoes into very thin slices--about 1/8-inch thick. Place them in a bowl and toss with 2 tablespoons of oil, half of thyme, and some salt and pepper.

2. Arrange the potato mixture in the bottom of a 9" x 13" baking pan. Bake for 25 minutes or until a golden and crispy brown.

3. Meanwhile, combine the bread crumbs, garlic, and remaining teaspoon of thyme. Place the cream in one shallow dish and the bread crumb mixture in another. Dip the fish fillet pieces, first in the cream, then in the bread crumb mixture. Coat both sides of the fish.

4. Heat oil in a large skillet and cook fish until golden and crispy on both sides and cooked through. Remove from the pan and place on paper towels. Cover with foil to keep warm.

5. When the potatoes are finished cooking, place the fish on top and serve. Sprinkle with parsley and serve with lemon wedges and a spot or two of ketchup.

Green Beans with Hazelnuts

SERVINGS: Enough for 6

1 1/2 pounds frozen French-style green beans
3 tablespoons butter
1/4 cup hazelnuts, coarsely chopped

WHAT TO DO:

1. Cook the green beans in the microwave oven according to the package directions.

2. In a skillet, melt the butter on top of the stove. When it starts to turn the color of nuts—be careful not to burn it—add the hazelnuts and stir-fry for about 30 seconds.

3. Combine the green beans and the nuts to serve.

Apricot-Kissed Apple Pie

Servings: Enough for 8

2 store-bought pie-crust disks
4 large apples, peeled, cored and thinly sliced
4 tablespoons butter
2 tablespoons sugar
Pinch of salt
Pinch of cinnamon
1/4 cup apricot jam, divided
1 egg yolk
1 tablespoon milk
Sugar for sprinkling

WHAT TO DO:

1. Preheat the oven to 450 degrees. Place the pie-crust disks on one or two cookie sheets--depending on size. Spread the center of each disk with half of the apricot jam, stopping short of the edge by about 1 inch.

2. In a bowl, pour the melted butter over the apples and mix. Sprinkle with the flour, sugar, salt, and cinnamon. Stir to distribute everything more or less evenly.

3. Mound half of the apples in the center of each pie crust, stopping short of the edge by 2 inches. Fold the edge over the apples, making pleats around the edges. The apples will be exposed in the center.

4. Mix the egg yolk with the milk. Brush any of the exposed pie crust with this mixture and sprinkle with sugar.. Bake for 20 minutes or until the pastry is nicely browned. Carefully slide off of the cookie sheets, and cool for half an hour on cooling racks.

6. In the microwave, melt any remaining apricot jam, and thin to a pouring consistency with a teaspoon of water. Glisten the apple tops with a few strokes of a brush dipped into this jam.

PACIFIC-RIM EATS

Salmon-from-a-Can Cakes

Roasted Carrots with Soy Sauce

Japanese Cucumber Salad

Flourless Orange Cake
with Citrus Compote

SALMON CAKES FROM A CAN

SERVINGS: Enough for 4

2 tablespoons oil
1/2 cup onion, chopped fine
7 1/2-ounce can salmon, drained
Small can chopped mild green chiles, drained
Pinch of ground cumin
2 tablespoons fresh cilantro
1/2 cup tortilla chips, crumbled
2 tablespoons flour
Ketchup

WHAT TO DO:

1. Heat 1 teaspoon of oil in a skillet. Add the onion and stir-fry for about 5 minutes. Cool the onion in a bowl and wipe the skillet clean with a paper towel.

2. Into the bowl with the cooling onions, add all of the remaining ingredients—except for the flour. Mix to combine and refrigerate for half an hour

3. Remove from refrigerator and shape into 1/2-inch-thick cakes.

4. Coat the salmon cakes with a dusting of flour. In the skillet, heat the remaining oil over high heat. Fry the salmon cakes until nicely browned on both sides—3 minutes per side.

5. Brush tops with Ketchup and serve.

ROASTED CARROTS WITH SOY SAUCE

SERVINGS: Enough for 4

1 pound carrots, peeled, quartered lengthwise, cut into 2-inch-long pieces
1 tablespoon vegetable oil
Salt to taste
1 tablespoon soy sauce
1 teaspoon fresh ginger, grated fine
2 teaspoons rice vinegar
1 teaspoon toasted sesame oil
2 teaspoons sesame seeds

WHAT TO DO:

1. Preheat oven to 450 degrees.

2. Toss the carrots with the vegetable oil. Sprinkle with salt and place in a roasting pan. Bake until tender, about 30 minutes.

3. Meanwhile, combine all of the remaining ingredients, except for the sesame seeds, in a medium bowl. Pour over the roasted carrots, toss together, sprinkle with the sesame seeds and serve.

JAPANESE CUCUMBER SALAD

SERVINGS: Enough for 4

3 cucumbers, slice paper thin
5 scallions, both green and white parts sliced thin
2 tablespoons rice vinegar
1/2 teaspoon sugar
Salt

WHAT TO DO:

Combine all the ingredients in a bowl. Cover and leave out to warm up to room temperature, up to an hour or so.

TIP: We like to use either Persian cucumbers or English Hot-House cucumbers for this and most of our other salads. Both of these cucumbers have paper thin skins that don't require peeling; we certainly never do.

FLOURLESS ORANGE CAKE WITH CITRUS COMPOTE

SERVINGS: Enough for 8

FOR THE CAKE

4 eggs, separated
1/2 cup plus 2 tablespoons granulated sugar, divided
2 oranges
1/4 pound almonds
1/2 teaspoon cinnamon
8-inch cake pan, lined with buttered and floured parchment paper
Confectioner's sugar for dusting cake

FOR THE COMPOTE

8 kumquats, sliced
4 oranges, peeled and cut into sections
2 tangerines, peeled and sectioned

WHAT TO DO:

1. Preheat oven to 350 degrees.

2. Finely grate the skin off of the two oranges and combine the skin with the sugar.
Beat the egg yolks and sugar until mixture is thick and pale. Fold in the rest of the cake ingredients.

3. In another bowl, beat the egg whites until stiff. Gently fold the beaten egg whites into the egg yolk mixture. Spoon the batter into a cake pan lined with parchment paper.

4. Bake for 45 minutes. Cool and dust with confectioner's sugar.

5. While the cake is baking, combine the fruit in a bowl. Sprinkle with some sugar. Leave at room temperature for one hour. Stir and serve with slices of the cake.

Lupe

In the out-door café of the Bowers Museum, Lupe and I sit over lunch surrounded by the Pre-Columbian Exhibits, The First Californians, and the Art of the Pacific Islands: Spirits and Headhunters. The collected force of the handwork of so many long-dead artists is pressing hard on our senses. The past is now. Lupe is on a roll with life advice: "Aim for good cycles [in life]." "Surrender yourself to God." The waiter re-filling the water glasses chimes in, "hold hands." "That too," Lupe dismisses the interruption and gets back to her favorite subject: her Mesoamerican ancestors and their collective DNA coursing through her blood. "My Mexican grandfather is in my mom's personality. He's in my humor," she says, to ex-plain. "Only the dead bury the dead." An interesting thought suggesting that only the living live with the dead. It makes for heady stuff, this stuff that Lupe regularly stokes with her readings—a constant stream of spiritual books and eagerly attended spiritual retreats. At home, to focus her mind on

God and her prayers, Lupe has set up an altar decorated with a handful of falcon feathers, a candle to light when she's "in the spiritual mood," and a statue of her name sake: The flame radiating Virgin of Guadalupe—the patron saint of Mexico. As busy as Lupe is at keeping open her pathways to the past and never saying good-bye to those who've been in her life, it is, however, her two-year-old toddler who's most recently had the most profound effects on the young mother's immediate life.

At two, Luisa is more mature than I was until just recently. She remembers her lessons; she won't touch things twice, once I tell her not to. She's the reason I stopped drinking, partying and smoking. She reunited me with her dad. She now lives with us: We are a functioning family. It's really exciting.

Joey keeps saying we should have another child, but what I want is to achieve some other goals: First, I'm graduating from UCI. In two quarters I will be the 1st generation college graduate in our family. Luisa will be a 2nd generation graduate. I also want Joey [Luisa's father] to go back to doing this amazing art that he does. His art is somewhat in the spirit of what you see here at the Bowers. It is amazing, I keep telling him. It's what made me fall in love with him in the first place. It's his real gift to the world. His work as a roofer, that's just temporary. I have other plans for him.

Right now, I'm investing 100 percent of my energy into my education. My next goal is to get my masters from the University of New Mexico. No, I've never been there but, from what I heard, it will be the perfect place for us to build our family life. I know that I want to pursue a career in education.

I want to be a school psychologist. I'm planning to be the breadwinner in my family. Joey and I are complete opposites—he's so talented. He will be known in the community for his great artistic abilities.

I keep seeing us in the Southwest, in a house with a horse for transportation. Of course, I don't know what it takes to take care of a horse, but we'll figure it out as we go. You're right, the house will need to be close to my job. But I know that I definitely don't want a car.

When I was in high school I really wanted to be an actress. I had a 15-count solo in "Hello Dolly" when I was at Santa Ana High School. I was in an improv. I had the lead in "The Bride." I liked the outfits. But what I really liked most is to be on stage. . . . I don't deny it: I'm a drama queen. Even off stage, it's who I am. I have my rights. I don't side step an issue. I have my opinions. And people will know about them. Just ask my neighbors.

The other day I started screaming at this guy who's about 30 with his under-aged girlfriend. They were hanging out around the corner of my building, looking like they were up to no good. Even though I live in a smoke-free building, my neighborhood is full of drug addicts—it's like the dead living around us. But they are not really dead. They're more like the undead--zombies in so many ways.

The only thing that scares me more than zombies is the thought of being caught in a Tsunami. True, that might be somewhat farfetched, living in Santa Ana. But being caught in gunfire as an innocent bystander is another one of my fears, and that's a very rational fear given where I live.

The most important thing other than family is to create a good social network. It's so important to be around positive people and to figure out how to combine those things that they offer in a way that makes most sense.

For me, in college, I started to connect my parents' oral traditions and my Catholic ideology with what I learned about the Tlaxcala systems [indigenous people who settled Central Mexico 12,000 to 6,000 years ago]. For some reason I also stared to realize what an important part good food plays in who we are.

Though it is basic, good food has become very important to me. What I really love is a great pizza, not the Pizza Hut type but something I make myself. It's more of a gourmet pizza that I make. I love when we make time to eat it together, and share stories, and enjoy the well being of being close, connected as a family.

My parents split up when I was in 6th grade. It was a great sadness, still is when I think of it: There were six of us children and our dad was no longer with us. When he met my mom, he already had another family, also with six kids. One day he went back to his first wife but that's another story. It's complicated.

I want my life uncomplicated. I'm really looking forward to that horse in the backyard, but right now my biggest fear is that I'm not on top of my laundry. There's always a growing mountain of clothes—my clothes, my girl's clothes, my boyfriends. When I get caught up, now that there's a break in school for me, I also want to get a little more sleep.

It's been so long since I've fallen into a dream cycle. I'm really looking forward to dreaming again. That, and there's my trip to Mexico. I'm going with a couple of high-school girlfriends and taking Luisa with me. It will be the first time for her. We'll be staying in one of my mom's apartments. I can't wait. I'm so excited. I just got our tickets.

Dulce

A year and a half ago, Dulce taped a Morning Garden flier to her refrigerator door; she looked at it everyday for the next two months before finally gathering up enough confidence to put her child in the stroller and take the short walk from her one-room apartment to the courtyard of the "Red Church" on the corner of North Bush Street and Civic Center Boulevard. Since then, she says, she's had a small series of

successes: None more surprising to her than her new ability to speak English.

Morning Garden gives me the confidence to try to speak English. Everywhere I go in Santa Ana, everyone speaks Spanish to me. So I never even try. Here, I discover that I can learn to speak and understand. My husband, when he heard me speak one day, he said, "Dulce, you surprise me how you speak English." And, I surprise myself too when I discover how much I can do— that I can learn so much.

I even learned how to crochet [here]. Now, I can make something with my hands that my kids can wear. They look so cute in their hats, and they are so proud that I make things for them.

When I was little, one teacher in Puebla gave me a book written by Gabriel Garcia Marquez. The name of the book is *Doce Cuentos Peregrinos* [Twelve Stories of Pilgrims]. I think it is my best treasure that I still have. And I think, because of this book, I still like to read and I want for my children to read too.

The best surprise in my life was when I became a mom. When you have a new baby everything changes forever. Now Amy is seven years old and Camila is 4 years old, and everyday I try to make life better for them. I think that is probably why I decided to go back to Mexico and live there.

It is for the success of my kids that I'm taking us back. I think Amy and Camila will have more opportunity in Mexico. Here, I look around and I see that the best they can do when they grow up is become a checker in a grocery store. In Mexico, I have more hope for them: that they will go to college; that they will have the education for a better profession.

When I was growing up, I dreamed about being a doctor. My grades in school were always good. I liked chemistry and anatomy. But my dad said to me, " I feel so bad for you Dulce, but there is no money." He suggested that I study to become a nurse, and that's what I did.

I tell my bigger daughter, "Amy, you can be whatever you want to be. " And she always says, "I know, Mom. But what do you want me to be?"

It is not a surprise to anyone that my dream is that she becomes a doctor. And, when we are back in Mexico, I think I will try to go back to school too for to study more nursing and to get a better job.

For me, a better job would be to work as a nurse--not in a hospital. Work in a hospital: There is so much stress all the time, and I don't work with stress. Stress makes me close up and I stop thinking, I know. When I worked in a hospital in Mexico, a friend told me, "I have work with an elderly person. I think you will like it. And the pay is good." She was right. The work was better for me. And the pay was better too.

For success, I have to know what I want. Now, what I want is enough money for the stability of my family. We never have enough. My husband now has two jobs: In the morning he does construction; at night he cleans a restaurant. It is too much work for one person. In Mexico, it's not expensive like here to live. We have a little house there. We have family.

The secret to a good live, I know, is not money. But it is necessary to have enough and not worry all the time. One time, I saw a documentary on TV about life in a small town in Sweden. It showed people living a very simple, traditional life. Everyone know everyone. They all worked in the fields growing food. Everyone was so happy. I don't know it that's possible. But is was so nice. It made me very happy. Maybe someday, I'll go and visit Sweden. Probably, when I see it, it won't be anything like the life they showed on TV.

The biggest fear in my life is to lose one of my children. I think that is because my brother was killed in an accident in Mexico. The police found him dead under a bridge. "Maybe somebody pushed him off his bicycle," the police said. No one saw how he died. It was a mystery. We never found out what happened, but my mother she has never recovered from the shock. It was the worst time for our family. That happened seven years ago.

The best advice I ever got is from my dad. He always says, "Never make decisions when you are angry. Don't let your anger speak."

The worst advice I ever got was in a clinic, here. The doctor told me that my blood tests suggested that my baby would be premature and she would be born with some syndrome. He advised me to have an abortion. My husband told me, "Go to another doctor." I changed the doctor and everything turned out fine. Camila was not premature and she is perfect.

I will be sad to leave Santa Ana. Now that I have my tickets to fly back to Mexico, I sometimes think that I would like to live here. But, I know, the best option for me is to return to where my kids will have more opportunity.

My husband? Yes, he will come to Mexico too. Later. And we will live like the people in a good story: Poor, happy, surrounded by our family.

Spring

artichokes

asparagus

beans, fava

cauliflower

lettuce

mushrooms, morel

peas

rhubarb

spinach

sorrel

strawberries

tamarind

zucchini blossoms

HOORAY FOR SPRING

Chicken-Kielbasa Paella

Grilled Flat Bread

Banana-Pudding Cake

Chicken-Kielbasa Paella

SERVINGS: Enough for 8

4 cups chicken stock
1/2 teaspoon ground saffron (or tablespoon tomato paste--for color)
Salt and pepper
8 chicken thighs (about 3 1/2 pounds), bone-in, skin-on
1 teaspoon smoked Spanish paprika
2 teaspoons oil
12 ounces Kielbasa sausage, 1/8-inch-thick slices
1 white onion, chopped
4 garlic cloves, minced
3 medium tomatoes, chopped coarsely
2 1/2 cups Arborio rice
1 cup frozen peas

WHAT TO DO:

1. Preheat the oven to 400 degrees.

2. In a saucepan over medium heat, warm the chicken stock, saffron, and about 1/2 teaspoon salt.

3. Season the chicken with 2 teaspoons salt, 1/2 teaspoon pepper, and the smoked paprika.

4. Heat the oil in a 14-inch paella pan or a high-sided ovenproof skillet. Over high heat, brown the chicken for 6 to 8 minutes and transfer the pieces to a plate.

3. In the same skillet, over medium/high heat, lightly brown the sliced sausage. Add onion and garlic, and cook an additional 5 minutes. Stir in the rice, add the chicken stock to the mixture, and bring to a boil. Cook for 2 minutes, stirring often. Add peas, chicken, and saffron.

4. Bake in the same skillet for 20 minutes. Let stand for 10 minutes before serving. Remember, the pan handle will be hot.

Grilled Flat Bread

SERVINGS: Makes 8 to 10 flat breads

1 tablespoon dry yeast
2 teaspoons sugar
1 cup water
1 tablespoon salt
4 cups flour
2 tablespoons oil
1/2 cup green onions, thinly sliced
1/4 cup parsley, coarsely chopped

WHAT TO DO:

1. In a standing mixer, combine the yeast, sugar, and water. Let the mixture rest in a warm place until foamy, about 10 minutes.

2. Add the oil to the mixture, followed with flour and salt. Mix until dough just starts coming together--don't overwork the mixture.

3. Brush the top of the dough with a little oil. Cover the bowl tightly, and let the dough rise at room temperature until it doubles in size, about 1 hour.

4. Punch the dough down. Take it out of the bowl and, on a lightly floured surface, separate the loaf into eight pieces. Shape each piece with the palms of your hands into 1/4-inch-thick flatbreads.

4. Cover each side of the flatbread with a scattering of green onions and parsley, pressing the topping into the dough with a light roll of a rolling pin. Brush with additional olive oil.

5. Using either an outdoor grill or a large skillet, grill until both sides are cooked, about 2 minutes per side. Serve warm.

Banana-Pudding Cake

SERVINGS: Enough for 8

1 package instant vanilla pudding
1 pound cake, cut into ¼-inch-thick slices
40 vanilla wafers
5 Oreo cookies, crushed
3/4 cup strawberry jam
3/4 cup Ricotta cheese
2 teaspoons sugar
2 bananas, sliced
Another handful of crushed vanilla wafers for the topping
White chocolate shavings for topping
Fresh mint leaves for topping

WHAT TO DO:

1. Prepare the pudding according to the package directions.

2. Mix the strawberry jam with the crushed Oreo cookies. Mix the Ricotta cheese with the sugar.

3. Cover a 7 x 11-inch baking dish with half of the pound cake slices. Press 20 vanilla wafers into the cake.

4. Dollop half of the strawberry jam mixture over the wafers. Follow this with half of the Ricotta mixture. Top with half of the banana slices and half of the pudding.

5. Repeat this layering with the remaining half of the ingredients.

6. Top with additional crushed vanilla wafers, shaved white chocolate, and mint. Chill before serving.

APRIL FOOLS' LUNCH

Tortilla Cannelloni
with Asparagus & Ham
Cherry Tomatoes in Lettuce Cups
Strawberry Fool

Tortilla Cannelloni with Asparagus & Ham

SERVINGS: Enough for 6

2 pounds fresh asparagus
12 tablespoons butter - divided
1 cup water
Salt
6 ounces Canadian bacon, chopped fine
3 cups milk
4 1/2 tablespoons flour
1 cup Parmesan, grated
1/8 teaspoon ground nutmeg
Flour tortillas – medium or small size

WHAT TO DO:

1. With a vegetable peeler, peel the tough green skin from the base of the asparagus spears. Cut the asparagus into 2-inch lengths.

2. Preheat the oven to 450 degrees. Generously butter a 10x12-inch baking pan.

3. Melt 4 tablespoons of the butter in a skillet, add the asparagus, sprinkle with salt, and brown the asparagus lightly for up to 5 minutes. Set aside to cool.

4. To make the sauce, in a separate pan, heat the milk over low heat until small bubbles form, but do not let it boil.

5. In the same skillet used for browning the asparagus, melt 6 tablespoons of the butter and add the flour, stirring constantly with a wooden spoon.

6. In ½ cup increments, add the hot milk, whisking in each addition until smooth before adding more liquid.

6. When all the milk has been worked in, reduce the heat, add a pinch of salt, and stir constantly until the sauce is as dense as thick cream.

7. Combine the ham with the chopped asparagus set aside in a bowl. Add to the ham and asparagus half of the sauce, 2/3 cup of the Parmesan, and the nutmeg. Mix well.

8. Spread 1 tablespoon of the reserved white sauce on a plate. Rotate a tortilla in the sauce to cover. Spread about 2 tablespoon of the asparagus mixture on top of the tortilla, and roll up, jelly-roll fashion, to form a cannelloni. Place the cannelloni in a baking pan, seam side facing down. Repeat this process with the remaining tortillas, adding sauce as needed, leaving enough sauce to pour a bit on top of the cannelloni.

9. Pour the remaining sauce over the dish, smoothing it with the back of a spoon and sprinkling the top with the remaining 1/3 cup of Parmesan. Dot the top with the remaining 2 tablespoons of butter.

10. Bake for 15 to 20 minutes, until a golden brown crust forms on top. Allow it to cool for 5 to 8 minutes before serving.

Cherry Tomatoes in Lettuce Cups

SERVINGS: Enough for 6

2 cups cherry tomatoes, cut in half
3 green onions, both green and white parts sliced thinly
Pinch of sugar
Salt and pepper
1 tablespoon lemon juice
Soft lettuce leaves such a Boston lettuce, to make individual serving cups

WHAT TO DO:

1. Sprinkle the tomatoes with a pinch of sugar. Set aside for half an hour.

2. When ready to serve, stir in the onions and lemon juice.

3. Season to taste with the salt and pepper.

4. Arrange individual servings in lettuce cups.

Morning Garden Comes to Your Table

Strawberry Fool

SERVINGS: Enough for 8

1 – 20-ounce package frozen strawberries, thawed
2 tablespoons sugar
1 tablespoon lemon juice
1 tablespoon Framboise or other liqueur
2 pints fresh strawberries, hulled and cut in half
2-3 cups plain yogurt

WHAT TO DO:

About 30 minutes before serving, add the sugar, lemon juice, and liqueur to the fresh strawberries. Gently stir to combine, and set aside at room temperature.

When ready to serve, mix the fresh strawberries with the thawed strawberries. Layer the berries with the yogurt in individual cups. Top each serving with a fresh strawberry half.

Morning Garden Comes to Your Table

LENTEN MEAL

Creamy Macaroni and Cheese

Baked Breadsticks

Broccoli Pesto

Orange & Pineapple Yogurt Sherbet
with Blackberries

Creamy Macaroni and Cheese

SERVINGS: Enough for 6

2 tablespoons butter
1 cup cottage cheese (not low fat)
2 cups whole milk
1 teaspoon dry mustard
Pinch of cayenne
Pinch of nutmeg
1/2 teaspoon salt
1/4 teaspoon pepper
1 pound sharp or extra-sharp cheddar cheese, grated
1/2 pound elbow macaroni, uncooked

WHAT TO DO:

1. Position the oven rack to the upper third of the oven, and preheat to 375 degrees. Use 1 teaspoon of the butter to coat a 9x9-inch baking pan.

2. In a blender, purée the cottage cheese, milk, dry mustard, cayenne, nutmeg, salt, and pepper together. In a large bowl combine the milk mixture, uncooked macaroni, and most of the cheese—reserving several tablespoons for sprinkling on top of the dish towards the end of the baking time. Pour into the prepared pan, cover tightly with foil and bake 30 minutes.

3. Uncover the pan, stir gently, and sprinkle with reserved cheese. Dot with butter, and bake an additional 30 minutes until browned. Let cool at least 15 minutes before serving.

Breadsticks

SERVINGS: Enough for 6

1 pound French-bread baguette
1/4 cup olive oil
Broccoli Pesto

WHAT TO DO:

1. Cut the bread into 6-inch lengths and halve lengthwise. Cut each half lengthwise into 1 1/4-inch-wide strips. Preheat oven to 350 degrees.

2. Brush tops of bread with olive oil.

3. Bake 15 minutes.

4. Serve with Broccoli Pesto (recipe on following page).

Broccoli Pesto

SERVINGS: Makes 3 cups

2 cups broccoli, cooked and chopped
1/2 cup olive oil
1/3 cup pine nuts
2 garlic cloves, minced
1/4 cup Parmesan cheese, grated
1/4 cup pecorino cheese or Parmesan cheese
1 teaspoon coarse kosher salt

WHAT TO DO:

1. Place the broccoli, olive oil, pine nuts, and garlic cloves in a food processor or blender.

2. Process until a paste forms, stopping often to push down ingredients from the side of the bowl.

3. Add the cheeses and salt. Process the mixture until smooth. Transfer to a bowl. Serve at room temperature with bread.

Orange & Pineapple Frozen Yogurt with Blackberries

SERVINGS: Enough for 8

6-ounce can frozen orange juice concentrate, thawed
1/4 cup confectioner's sugar
2 cups canned crushed pineapple, drained
2 cups unflavored yogurt
2 oranges, peeled and thinly sliced
1 cup blackberries

WHAT TO DO:

1. Line a loaf pan with plastic wrap.

2. In a bowl, stir together the orange juice with the confectioner's sugar. Add the crushed pineapple and the yogurt, mixing thoroughly.

3. Pour the mixture into the lined loaf pan, cover, and freeze overnight.

4. When ready to serve, slice the frozen sherbet into thick slices and garnish with the oranges and blackberries.

COURTYARD FETE

Turkey and Sweet Corn Slider
Roasted Bell Pepper Coulis
Cabbage Slaw
Terrine of Ice-cream Sandwiches

God is great and God is good,
Let us thank God for our food.
Amen.

TRADITIONAL AMERICAN GRACE

Turkey and Sweet Corn Sliders

SERVINGS: Enough for 6

3 slices Italian bread, torn into pieces to yield one cup
1/3 cup milk
3 ounces sliced bacon, finely chopped
1 small onion, finely chopped
1 small clove garlic, minced
Salt and pepper
2 tablespoons oil
1 large egg
1 pound ground turkey
1/2 cup corn, canned
3 tablespoons fresh parsley, minced
1 tablespoon tomato paste
12 mini buns
Related Recipe: Roasted Pepper Coulis

WHAT TO DO:

1. Preheat oven to 400 degrees.

2. In a small bowl, soak the bread in milk until softened, about 4 minutes.

3. In a skillet over medium heat a touch of the oil. Cook the bacon, onion, and garlic with 1/2 teaspoon salt for about 5 minutes. Cool in a bowl.

4. Squeeze the moisture out of the bread. Discard the excess milk.

5. In a large bowl, lightly beat the egg, add the turkey, corn, bacon mixture, bread, and parsley. Mix well with your hands and form 12 meatballs. Arrange in a rimmed sheet pan.

6. Stir together the tomato paste and remaining 1 tablespoon of oil and brush over meatballs. Bake until just cooked through, 15 to 20 minutes.

7. Serve on mini buns accompanied with Roasted Bell Pepper Coulis (recipe on following page).

Roasted Bell Pepper Coulis

SERVINGS: Makes 3 cups

4 red bell peppers
2 tablespoons olive oil
2 shallots, finely chopped
2 cloves garlic, minced
1 1/2 cups vegetable stock or chicken broth
1/2 teaspoon sugar
1/2 teaspoon salt
1/4 teaspoon pepper

WHAT TO DO:

1. Roast the peppers on a grill or under the broiler or on the flame of a gas stove. Blacken all sides of the peppers. Place in a bowl and cover with plastic wrap. Allow the steam to loosen the skins. When cool enough to handle, rub the skin off with fingers. Rinse with cold water to get off the last bits of blackened skin. Cut off the top of the peppers and slice lengthwise. Cut out the white membranes and scrape away the seeds. Chop coarsely and set aside.

2. Heat the oil in a medium size sauté pan over medium-high heat. Add the shallots, lower the heat to medium, and sauté until soft and translucent, about 5 minutes. Add the garlic and sauté an additional minute, until fragrant.

3. Add the roasted red peppers and continue to sauté until they are heated through and the shallots are very soft, about 3 minutes more. Add the broth and sugar and cook, stirring, until nearly all the liquid has evaporated and the mixture is almost dry.

4. Spoon the mixture into a food processor fitted with a metal blade. Puree the mixture. Season with salt and pepper, to taste.

Cabbage Slaw

4 cups green cabbage, shredded
2 tablespoons white wine vinegar
1 cup carrots, shredded
1 1/2 cups apples, peeled, cored and coarsely grated
2 green onions, chopped fine
1 cup frozen corn, thawed
1/4 cup fresh cilantro, minced
2 teaspoons sugar
1/4 cup mayonnaise
1/4 cup sour cream
2 tablespoons canned chipotle chiles in adobo sauce, chopped fine
2 tablespoons fresh lime juice
Salt

WHAT TO DO:

1. Bring to boil the vinegar in the microwave along with 2 tablespoons of water. Pour over the shredded cabbage and mix to combine. Cover and marinate for at least 6 hours, or overnight in the refrigerator.

2. Strain the marinated cabbage and, in a large bowl, combine it with the cabbage, carrots, apples, green onions, corn, and cilantro.

3. In a small bowl, whisk together the sugar, mayonnaise, sour cream, chiles, and lime juice.

4. Pour the dressing over the slaw mixture and stir until combined. Season to taste with salt.

Terrine of Ice-Cream Sandwiches

This is easy, fast, and a sure crowd pleaser. Just keep in mind: It's not junk food, if you made it yourself.

SERVINGS: Enough for 6

Frozen Ice Cream Sandwiches
Kool whip
Chocolate sauce

WHAT TO DO:

1. Line an 8x12 dish with a layer of ice-cream sandwiches, cutting them to fit snuggly in the dish.

2. Spread a generous layer of Kool Whip over the ice-cream sandwiches.

3. Squiggle some chocolate lines over the cream. For a more "marbled" effect, drag a knife tip through the chocolate a couple of times.

4. Cut and serve.

TIP: For more color contrast and a touch of wow factor, serve with a strawberry along the side.

Morning Garden Comes to Your Table

EAT-OUT-OF-HAND MUNCHIES

Spring Rolls with Fishy Sauce
Egg Salad Sandwiches
Tuna Salad Wraps
No-Bake Frozen S'Mores Bars

Spring Rolls with Fishy Sauce

SERVINGS: Enough for 8

FOR THE SPRING ROLLS

2 ounces rice noodles
8 (9-inch) rice wrappers
8 large cooked shrimp, peeled and cut in half length wise
1 tablespoon fresh Thai basil, chopped fine
3 tablespoons fresh cilantro, chopped fine
3 tablespoons fresh mint leaves, minced
2 large lettuce leaves, cut fine into long strips

FOR THE DIPPING SAUCE

1 tablespoon fish sauce (available in the Asian section of the super market)
1/4 cup water
2 tablespoons fresh lime juice
1 clove garlic, minced
1 tablespoon sugar
1/4 teaspoon chili sauce
1 teaspoon toasted sesame oil
1 tablespoon soy sauce

WHAT TO DO:

1. In a small bowl, mix the dipping sauce ingredients. Set aside.

2. Bring a medium saucepan of water to boil. Boil rice vermicelli 3 to 5 minutes and drain.

3. In a bowl, combine the vermicelli with the chopped herbs and lettuce.

4. Fill a large bowl with warm water. Dip a rice wrapper into the hot water for 1 second to soften. Lay the wrapper flat.

5. Place a handful of herbs and vermicelli across the center of the wrapper and top with two halves of shrimp.

6. Fold the sides inward, and tightly roll the wrapper into a cylinder.

7. Serve with dipping sauce.

Egg Salad Sandwiches

SERVINGS: Enough for 6

8 large hard-boiled eggs
1/3 cup celery, finely chopped
1/4 cup pimiento-stuffed green olives, minced
1/2 cup mayonnaise
1 tablespoon Dijon mustard
1 tablespoon minced herbs such as parsley, chives, tarragon
12 bread slices

WHAT TO DO:

Peel and chop the eggs and combine with the rest of the ingredients.
Spread mixture on bread to create sandwiches. Cut into squares, dip points in minced herbs.

Tuna Salad Wraps

SERVINGS: Enough for 6
1/4 cup mayonnaise
2 tablespoons fresh lemon juice
2 – 6-ounce cans light tuna packed in olive oil, drained
1/2 cup canned roasted red peppers, drained and chopped
1 large celery rib, chopped fine
3 tablespoons red onion, chopped fine
Soft lettuce leaves for wrapping

WHAT TO DO:

1. In a large bowl, whisk together the mayonnaise and lemon juice.
Add the tuna, peppers, celery, and red onion, and stir together gently. Season to taste with salt and pepper.

2. Serve wrapped in lettuce leaves.

No-Bake Frozen S'Mores Bars

SERVINGS: Makes 12 bars

1/2 cup heavy cream
1 1/4 cup chocolate chips
2 cups miniature marshmallows
12 chocolate-covered graham crackers, broken up into small pieces
2 cups yogurt
1/2 teaspoon vanilla
Cinnamon graham cracker crumbs—for garnish

WHAT TO DO:

1. Heat cream in a saucepan for 2 minutes—don't bring it to boil.

2. Remove from heat. Add chocolate chips, stirring until they melt.

3. Add the yogurt and stir in the vanilla as well as the marshmallows and the chocolate graham cracker pieces.

4. Line a baking pan with foil, pour out the s'more mixture, sprinkle with cinnamon cracker crumbs, and freeze for 2 hours.

5. After the 2 hour freeze, cut into bars and keep frozen to serve as needed.

LATIN SPICE IS NICE

Chicken Enchiladas in Green Salsa

Cinnamon Bread Hearts

Banana Pudding with Tropical Fruit

Chicken Enchiladas in Green Salsa

THE GREEN SALSA

2 pounds tomatillos, husked, washed and chopped
2 jalapenos, seeded
3 small garlic cloves, minced
1 teaspoon ground cumin
1 bunch cilantro
1 tablespoon vegetable oil
1 tablespoon salt, or to taste

THE CHICKEN ENCHILADAS

3 Poblano chiles
1 cup heavy cream
16 – 6-inch-size corn tortillas
1/4 cup vegetable oil
4 cups cooked chicken, shredded
1 1/2 cups Muenster cheese, grated
4 cups Green Salsa, divided (recipe below)
1/2 cup green onion, chopped
1/4 cup cilantro, chopped

WHAT TO DO:

FOR THE GREEN SALSA

1. Put the tomatillos and jalapenos in a medium saucepan, and pour in enough cold water to barely cover (about 3 1/2 cups), and bring to a boil. Cook until jalapenos are soft and tomatillos are tender, about 20 minutes. Remove from heat, and let stand for 15 minutes.

2. Drain the mixture in a colander.

3. Wipe out the saucepan and set aside.

4. Put the tomatillos, jalapenos, garlic, and cumin in a blender and blend for a few seconds, just until the tomatillos are coarsely chopped. Adding the cilantro, stem ends first, Blend until the sauce is smooth and speckled with finely chopped cilantro. Don't over blend, however, or you will grind the tomatillo seeds and make the sauce thick and pasty rather than smooth and shiny. Taste, and season with salt.

5. Refrigerate until needed for up to a week: Now that you have a truly great green sauce, you can proceed with making the enchiladas as your schedule permits.

FOR THE ENCHILADAS

6. Preheat the oven to 375 degrees.

7. Pour 2 cups of the Green Salsa into a blender. Add the poblano chiles, and blend at low speed until smooth. Pour into a medium saucepan, and add the remaining Green Salsa and cream. Bring to a simmer over low heat. Remove from heat.

8. In a lightly oiled hot skillet soften the tortillas for 15 seconds on each side. Wrap in foil and keep warm, as you make the enchiladas.

9. Place 1/3 cup of the chicken on each tortilla. Roll to form an enchilada, and place it seam side down in a 9-by-13-inch baking dish. (This can be prepared up to 4 hours in advance: Just cover with a damp kitchen towel and plastic wrap, and refrigerate. Remove 30 minutes before baking.)

10. Pour the warmed salsa and cream sauce over the enchiladas. Jiggle the dish so the sauce settles in between the enchiladas.

11. Sprinkle the cheese evenly over the top. Bake until the sauce around the edges bubbles and the cheese is golden brown, about 20 minutes. Allow 5 minutes of standing time before serving.

12. Scatter the onion and cilantro over the enchiladas before serving.

Cinnamon Bread Hearts

You will need a large heart shaped cookie cutter for cutting the bread into these almost instant cookies.

SERVINGS: Use one piece of bread for each serving

Sliced white bread
Butter, melted
1/2 cup sugar
Cinnamon to taste

WHAT TO DO:

1. Cut bread slices with the cookie cutter, reserving the cut away bread for bread crumbs.

2. Brush each heart with butter and sprinkle the tops with a mixture of cinnamon and sugar.

3. Toast in a toaster oven until sugar is bubbly.

Coconut Pudding with Tropical Fruit

SERVINGS: Enough for 4

1 package instant vanilla pudding
2 cups milk
1/2 cup unsweetened, flaked coconut, plus more for topping
1/2 cup pineapple, peeled, cored and diced
1/2 cup banana, cubed
1/2 cup papaya, peeled, chopped and pureed

WHAT TO DO:

1. Prepare the pudding according to the package directions. Stir in the coconut.

2. In a bowl, combine the pineapple with the bananas and the papaya purée.

3. Divide half of the fruit mixture among 4 wine glasses. Top with the pudding and then the remaining fruit.

4. Chill until cold, about 1 hour.

5. Sprinkle with additional coconut, baked in a 350-degree oven for a few minutes until lightly browned.

Morning Garden Comes to Your Table

VEGETARIAN SPRING FLING

Green Goddess Salad with Deviled Eggs

Three-Types-of-Beans Salad

Strawberry Sandwiches

Brazilian Lemonade

Green Goddess Salad
with Deviled Eggs

SERVINGS: Enough for 8

FOR THE SALAD

3 pounds new potatoes, boiled until tender in skins
1 cup cherry tomatoes, halved

FOR THE DRESSING
1 1/2 cup mayonnaise
4 salted anchovy fillets
2 green onions, green and white parts
2 tablespoons fresh tarragon
2 tablespoons fresh chives
2 tablespoons fresh parsley
2 tablespoons vinegar or lemon juice

FOR THE DEVILED EGGS
12 large eggs
1/3 cup mayonnaise
2 to 3 teaspoons canned chipotle chiles, drained and finely chopped
24 fresh cilantro leaves
Herb flowers: cilantro, arugula, chives

WHAT TO DO:

1. Make the salad dressing by pulsing all the ingredients in a food processor, to make a rough puree.

2. Combine about half of the dressing with the boiled potatoes, cut into 1-inch chunks. Refrigerate until ready to serve. (Reserve the rest of the dressing for other uses.)

3. To make the deviled eggs: Place the 12 eggs in a large saucepan, and add enough cold water to cover. Bring to a simmer over high heat. Reduce heat to low, and simmer gently for 5 minutes. Remove from heat, cover, and let stand 10 minutes. Drain eggs and cover with ice and water. Let stand until cold.

4. Peel the eggs and cut in half lengthwise. Spoon the yolks into a small bowl. Arrange the whites on a platter.

5. Mash the yolks with a fork and press them with the back of a spoon through a medium grid strainer into a bowl. Press the chiles through the same strainer, and mix in the mayonnaise in the bowl. Season to taste with salt.

6. Using a pastry bag fitted with a ½-inch-diameter star tip, pipe filling into egg whites. Cover and chill the filled eggs up to one day.

7. When ready to serve: Press 1 cilantro leaf into each egg and decorate with herb flowers. Serve along with the potato salad covered with cherry tomato halves.

We ask you for what we want,
And in Your divine extravagance,
You give us what we need.
Thank you, Lord.

Lord Jesus be our holy guest,
Our morning joy, our evening rest.
And with our daily bread impart,
Thy loving peace to every heart.

TRADITIONAL AMERICAN GRACE

Three-Types-of-Beans Salad

SERVINGS: Enough for 12

1/3 cup olive oil
1/4 cup white wine vinegar
1 tablespoon sugar
1 1/2 teaspoons dried oregano
15 to 16 ounce can kidney beans, drained and rinsed
15 to 16 ounce can garbanzo beans, drained and rinsed
15 to 16 ounce can black-eyed peas, drained and rinsed
1 cup green bell pepper, diced fine
1 cup red bell pepper, diced fine
1 cup pimiento-stuffed olives
1/2 cup red onion, chopped fine
Soft leaved lettuce

WHAT TO DO:

1. In a large bowl, whisk together the olive oil, vinegar, sugar, and oregano.

2. Add all remaining ingredients and toss to blend. Season to taste with salt and pepper.

3. Cover and refrigerate at least 3 hours and up to 1 day.

TIP: We like to serve this cupped inside of soft lettuce leaves.

Strawberry Sandwiches

SERVINGS: Enough for 2

2 slices white bread
1 tablespoon cream cheese
2 to 3 strawberries, hulled and sliced
2 ounces semi-sweet chocolate

WHAT TO DO:

1. Toast the bread. Spread the toast with cream cheese. Arrange overlapping slices of strawberries. Cover with the second piece of toast.

2. Cut the sandwich into 4 triangles.

3. Melt the chocolate in the microwave oven.

4. Dip the corners of the sandwiches into the melted chocolate.

TIP: Blend a bit of melted chocolate with some softened cream cheese to create an outrageously yummy spread.

3 ounces cream cheese, softened
3 tablespoons milk
2 cups confectioners' sugar
3 oz. unsweetened chocolate, melted
Pinch of salt

Beat everything together and use as a spread on toasted bread.

Brazilian Lemonade

SERVINGS: Makes 6 cups

1/2 cup brown sugar
1/2 cup water
3 limes, cut in quarters
3 tablespoons sweetened condensed milk
Additional water

WHAT TO DO:

1. Bring to a boil the equal amounts of sugar and water. Stir until the sugar dissolves. Pour into a pitcher and set aside to cool.

2. Place the limes (with the peels still on) and the condensed milk into a blender. Add 4 cups of cold water and blend on high speed until limes are slightly chopped.

3. Pour the lime mixture through a strainer into the pitcher with the sugar syrup.

4. Stir and taste. Dilute with additional water to suit individual taste.

PASTICHE OF FLAVORS

Crab Cakes

Linguini with Cauliflower and Olives

Strawberries and Oranges

Our Best Chocolate Cookies

Crab Cakes

SERVINGS: Enough for 6

1 pound pasteurized crab meat, best quality
1/2 pound fish such as cod, hake, tilapia—chopped
Few dashes of hot sauce
1 teaspoon fresh lemon peel, finely grated
1/2 cup mayonnaise
1/4 cup green onions, finely sliced
2 tablespoons fresh parsley, minced
Salt and pepper
1 cup bread crumbs—homemade are best, but any will work
Butter for browning

WHAT TO DO:

1. Combine everything except the bread crumbs in a bowl.

2. Scatter the bread crumbs evenly on a cookie sheet.

3. Shape the crab mixture into 6 or 8 patties, and lay them on the cookie sheet.

4. Gather all the exposed crumbs up from around the crab cakes and press them gently over the tops to make a thick coating.

5. Refrigerate on the cookie sheet for at least 30 minutes, up to 3 hours.

6. When ready to serve, melt some butter in a large skillet. When hot, take the crab cakes out of the refrigerator as needed and brown them on both sides—about 3 minutes per side. Keep warm in a 300 degree oven.

7. Serve with any sauce. We suggest the following: Whisk together ½ mayonnaise, 2 tablespoons fresh lemon juice, drops of hot sauce, and chopped parsley.

Linguine with Cauliflower and Olives

SERVINGS: Enough for 6

1 1/4 cups pitted brine-cured green olives
1/2 cup parsley, chopped
1/2 cup olive oil
1 large head cauliflower, cut into florets
1/2 teaspoon salt
3 garlic cloves, finely chopped
Pinch of red-pepper flakes
1 pound linguine
2 ounces Parmesan, grated
1 cup almonds, toasted and coarsely chopped

WHAT TO DO:

1. Pulse the olives and parsley in a food processor to chop coarsely. Set aside in a bowl.

2. Cook the cauliflower in boiling water for about 4 minutes. Fish the cooked cauliflower out of the pot with a slotted spoon and allow to cool in a bowl.

3. Bring the cauliflower water in the pot to a boil once more, stir in the pasta, cover the pot, and allow the pasta to cook itself by setting the pot aside--off the heat--for 15 minutes.

4. In a large skillet, heat the oil and sauté the cauliflower until a bit golden. Add the garlic and red-pepper flakes. Stir in a ½ cup of hot pasta water as well as the chopped olives and parsley and keep at a simmer until ready to mix with the cooked, drained pasta. Serve sprinkled with the almonds and the Parmesan cheese.

TIP: You might be tempted to cut down on the green olives here, but we don't advise it: The balance of these ingredients registered just about perfect on our palates.

Our Best Chocolate Cookies

Moist, tender, intensely chocolatey, deliciously nutty: Every time we make these, everyone wants the recipe—even those who profess to detest nuts in their cookies.

SERVINGS: 24 large cookies

1 stick unsalted butter (8 tablespoons)
9 ounces semisweet chocolate, finely chopped
3 ounces unsweetened chocolate, finely chopped
1/2 cup flour
1/2 teaspoon baking powder
Pinch of salt
3 eggs at room temperature
1 1/4 cup sugar
2 teaspoons vanilla
2 cups chocolate chips
2 cups pecans or walnuts, coarsely chopped

WHAT TO DO:

Preheat oven to 350 degrees.

1. Line two cookie sheets with parchment paper.

2. Melt the butter in a double boiler. Add both of the chopped chocolates to the hot butter. Cover the bowl with a lid. Stir after five minutes to create a smooth mixture. Set aside.

3. Sift the flour with the salt and baking powder into a bowl.

4. Whip the eggs in the bowl of a standing mixer for about one minute. Increase the speed to high as you gradually add the sugar and vanilla. Beat, at medium/high speed for a total of 4 minutes.

5. Reduce the speed and mix in the tepid chocolate until no streaks remain.

6. At this point, at very low speed, add the flour mixture just to combine.

7. Remove the bowl from the mixer and with a wooden spoon, by hand, stir in the chocolate chips and nuts.

8. Using an ice-cream scoop, place 2-inches apart mounds of batter on the cookie sheets.

9. Bake for no longer than 20 minutes.

10. Even if after that time, the cookies appear under baked, take them out of the oven and cool completely on the cookie sheets.

TIP: The nuts are an integral part of the structure of these cookies. So, if you're adverse to eating nuts, we suggest you try another chocolate cookie recipe.

From Carol's Perspective

Morning Garden has its roots in a childhood friendship
reaching back to when Father Brad and I were five years old. After sharing
graham crackers and milk in kindergarten for a year, we remained friends
for the next twelve years of school.

Our friendship rekindled forty years later in 2003 when I returned from
Canada to live in Santa Ana, and visited Father Brad at the Messiah Episcopal Church in the downtown core where he had been ministering for nearly

three decades. By then I had been a Waldorf early childhood teacher for many years.

One day in January 2007, I read a message Father Brad wrote in the Messiah Church newsletter. Writing that he wanted to increase the commitment of his parish to the homeless families in the downtown core of Santa Ana, he said he wanted in particular to create something for the families who were staying at the Isaiah House shelter with very young children.

Reading his words, I could not stop thinking about it for weeks. I began to imagine a way I might share my energy and my early childhood teaching experience with these families. I called Father Brad and offered to open a weekly parent-child program for the families with young children. Father Brad was delighted and suggested that we use the Nursery room and adjacent courtyard at the church. We delivered invitations to the families at Isaiah House, and Morning Garden was born in February 2007.

My vision was to create a simple and welcoming atmosphere where the children could unwind from the stress of street and shelter life and just be little children for a morning. I envisioned a homelike program with no explicit educational agenda, a place where parents and children could play and eat together for one morning each week.

In the beginning Morning Garden met on Tuesday mornings with parents and children together in the same room. As time passed, we decided to create a separate program for the parents, and in September 2007, Morning Garden expanded from one day to three days a week.

While two of us met with the children in a preschool program on Monday, Tuesday and Wednesday mornings, the mothers pursued their own activities; film and discussion on Mondays, crafting on Tuesdays, and the preparation of a full course meal for all of us on Wednesdays.

The idea for an entire morning of cooking had occurred to me during the early weeks of Morning Garden, after visiting Isaiah House when the homeless families gathered for their evening meal. The food was prepared and served by volunteers. Families filed through the kitchen to pick up their meals on paper plates, and walked outside to eat their meal. The grown-ups sat side by side on a low wall, which surrounded a patio.

As the parents ate, balancing their plates and cups on their laps, their children ran around the patio playing and taking a few bites of food. Eating with the families, I thought to myself: What if these moms had a place where they could cook for their children? What if they could eat together around a table with dishes and a tablecloth? Could we do this at Morning Garden?

When parents prepare and serve a meal to their children, they are expressing love and care in a tangible way. Eating as a family anchors children and gives them a sense of belonging. I thought it would make a difference for these transient families to have a settled time of cooking and eating together at a beautiful table, even for just one day a week.

We would need someone to help the mothers plan the meals, cook the food, and prepare the table. I thought of my friend Lucy who had a talent for creating delicious meals and serving them in a gracious way. I knew Lucy would have the culinary skill and the imagination to make a family meal-time happen. When asked, Lucy stepped up with enthusiasm to the task of organizing and leading the mothers in a cooking adventure.

A mealtime ritual can bring a profound sense of order and wellbeing to children. Sitting around a table to eat together, we experience one another's genuine presence. Laying down a tablecloth, setting out plates and cutlery, lighting a candle, and serving one another from a common bowl brings us together on a basic level and allows us to spend precious time together. We have an opportunity to look into each other's eyes and listen to each another talk about the events of the day.

As the weeks rolled by, I noticed a visible sense of confidence growing in the mothers and children alike. It was wonderful to see Lucy carrying the bags of groceries to the kitchen early on Wednesday mornings, to watch the mothers chopping and grating, stirring and baking as the meal came together. The mouth-watering aromas of lunch reached us upstairs in the preschool room. Finally, at the end of the morning a messenger would come knocking on our door to announce, "Lunch Is Ready!"

We formed a long lunch train of hungry children and sang our way through the courtyard and down the stairs to the kitchen and parish hall. Gathering around the table, we listened to Father Brad say the blessing before devouring another delicious lunch made from scratch by Lucy and the moms.

Morning Garden has grown and blossomed since those early days. It is now part of Hands Together Child Care Centre and has expanded its horizons to include working mothers. The pre-school program is still thriving, along with adult training programs. The cooking and eating together remain a central part of the week for the families who attend.

Morning Garden Comes to Your Table is Lucy's record of the delicious seasonal meals that were prepared and served at Morning Garden for four years. It is a reminder that eating together at a common table brings us together in communion with each other.

Carol Nasr Griset
Halifax, Nova Scotia

In fellowship assembled here,
We thank thee, Lord, for food and cheer
And through our Saviour, thy dear Son,
We pray, " God bless us, every one."

Charles Dickens

From Father Brad's Perspective

When my host, Dwight Smith, invited me into the rambling old craftsman home in a Santa Ana barrio neighborhood, I encountered several mothers and children moving sleeping pads off the old wooden floor. All the furniture had been removed to make room for the homeless families that found last-resort shelter here at the Isaiah House of the Catholic Worker. As Dwight and I walked through the rooms toward the back yard, oatmeal simmered in a huge pot on an old kitchen stove.

"We often have 100 mothers and children staying with us, here in the house or in tent shelters in the backyard," Dwight said. " The families have to be out of the building during the day, under orders from the City of Santa Ana. School aged children are brought to the County school in Orange, but I have a big problem with the mothers who have preschool aged children. There is nothing for them, so they go to the park. That's not a safe environment. I know that you're working with Hands Together---a Center for Children. I really need your help to create some program for these little children."

Dwight and I have been friends for many years, as Catholic Worker has cooked the main daily meal they distribute at the Civic Center in the kitchen at Messiah Episcopal Church where I have been the pastor. But this was a difficult challenge. I was running into dead ends. I shared the dilemma in our parish newsletter and then a wonderful thing happened.

My lifelong friend Carol Nasr Griset had recently moved to Santa Ana after living many years in Nova Scotia. Carol and I were in kindergarten in Pasadena and went through most of our school years together in the same classes. Carol is an experienced early childhood educator from the Waldorf system and has a real heart for the poor. She called me and expressed interest in this challenge. We visited the Isaiah House together and could see the children running about and the potential of some program of early childhood education and parenting support. We could see that these young mothers needed help in learning how to mother a child without the sheltering benefits provided by a constant home.

In a few weeks, Carol began a pilot program at the parish. New wooden child-size furniture was purchased by the church, in line with the Waldorf philosophy of using all natural materials. I will never forget this scene: I entered the little classroom. The children had finished their play time and gathered around a little table, Carol on one side. She held a warm face cloth scented with lavender. She wiped the hands and face of each child with a separate towel. I later learned that the lavender has a calming effect. On a corner of the table was a candle holder with the figure of a squirrel and the warm yellow glow of a flame. Carol and I joined hands with the children and sang a song. Warm apple sauce, crackers and cheese, and fruit juice were distributed. The children's energetic play was now calmed and they quietly ate the snacks: Candlelight reflecting of their faces; the scent lavender caressing the room.

As Carol's program expanded and she developed trusting relationships with the children, others noticed. Volunteers came on board, including a child psychiatrist and family therapist who worked with the mothers on the challenges of parenting in dire poverty.

Over the years Morning Garden has expanded, with new staff and many new mothers. This unique program for preschool aged children who have spent their entire lives in temporary shelter may be the only one of its kind in Orange County.

We pray that God will continue to smile on our efforts and provide the nurturing support and fellowship to make Morning Garden continue to prosper and grow.

Father Brad Karelius
Rector (retired), Messiah Episcopal Church
Santa Ana, California

G

H-I-J

K-L

M

MEAT

May the road rise up to meet you,
May the wind be at your back,
May good friends be there to greet you,
And your table never lack.

May your life be filled with laughter,
And you heart be filled with song.
May God shine His light upon you,
As you live your whole life long.

TRADITIONAL IRISH BLESSING